The Shabbat Effect

Jewish Wisdom for Growth and Transformation

Alan Morinis

BLOOMSBURY ACADEMIC

NEW YORK · LONDON · OXFORD · NEW DELHI · SYDNEY

BLOOMSBURY ACADEMIC
Bloomsbury Publishing Inc
1359 Broadway, 12th Floor, New York, NY 10018, USA
50 Bedford Square, London, WC1B 3DP, UK
29 Earlsfort Terrace, Dublin 2, Ireland

BLOOMSBURY, BLOOMSBURY ACADEMIC and the Diana logo are trademarks of
Bloomsbury Publishing Plc

First published in the United States of America 2026

A catalog record for this book is available from the Library of Congress.

Library of Congress Control Number: 2025945563

ISBN: HB: 979-8-8818-0787-0
ePDF: 979-8-7651-6524-9
eBook: 979-8-8818-0788-7

Typeset by Deanta Global Publishing Services, Chennai, India
Printed and bound in the United States of America

To find out more about our authors and books visit www.bloomsbury.com and
sign up for our newsletters.

*To all my many and diverse friends and colleagues at
The Mussar Institute who serve faithfully to make the wisdom
of Mussar more available in our time.*

Contents

Acknowledgments

I am forever indebted to Rabbi Yechiel Yitzchok Perr, z"l, and Rebbetzin Shoshana Perr for their loving guidance on the path of Mussar and of life itself, and to the extended Perr family, all of whom have made me feel a *ben bayit*, a son of their house, where I experienced my first real Shabbat.

Great gratitude is due to the One Above for giving me my wife, Dr. Bev Spring, and children, Dr. Julia Orkin and Dr. Leora Morinis, who are part of me, the part that balances and sustains me.

This book owes much to my dear friend Rabbi Micha Berger, who was my partner in germinating the concept. I have learned so much from Micha and continue to add to the debt I owe him. He is a treasured friend.

I would not have been able to write this book without the partnership of Rabbi Avi Fertig who, by taking on the leadership of programming for The Mussar Institute, has freed me to be able to write. But, in truth, that represents only a fraction of what I have to be grateful for regarding Avi, who is my friend, *chevruta*, travel companion, confidante, teacher, and beloved spiritual brother.

This book is dedicated to my colleagues and friends at the Mussar Institute, my true community, the people among whom I am happiest and most fulfilled of any of my communities, people who share my belief that the possibility of holiness that the universe whispers is, in fact, true, and we only need to get on with doing the work. I hold special regard and gratitude for my students, especially those who took the journey of learning that resulted in this book, because they have taught me so much.

Richard Brown at Bloomsbury has been an exemplary editor for me, respecting that this is my work as author, and also offering so much guidance from his vast experience to help it find its best possible expression and its best route out into the world.

I also acknowledge my agent, Jim Levine, who didn't feel this book was quite right for him but nevertheless continued to generously give help and support that proved invaluable for bringing it to the light of day.

My heart cannot contain the full extent of the gratitude I feel toward the masters of Mussar from previous centuries who delved with curiosity and honesty into the nature of the human condition and who passed down to us their wisdom and practical lessons, so that we, their spiritual descendants, can live lives that align more closely with our highest, God-given potential.

A Note on Practice

The Shabbat effect doesn't happen just because you turn off your phone or say the requisite prayers. The dividend of a Shabbat practice is paid out when you maintain a day of rest with the conscious intention of developing the character traits outlined in this book, and perhaps others as well.

How to practice Shabbat itself is not a subject for this book. There are many other sources that go into great detail on the guidelines for building an effective day of rest according to Jewish principles. The practice that concerns us here has to do with ensuring that your Shabbat is never a rote performance but rather a *living* experience that, step by step, brings about a spiritual transformation.

I'll mention briefly here a process to which I will return in the Conclusion, which is called *hitlamdut*, a Hebrew term that means "teaching yourself," or, as I have also heard it called, "reflexive learning." Practicing *hitlamdut* means approaching every experience with the attitude that you are a student of your own life, seeking the lessons embedded in every situation in which you find yourself.

Practicing *hitlamdut* on Shabbat means analyzing your experiences in search of lessons about your own awareness, harmony, rest, and the other inner traits that are examined in this book, both those that come easily to you and those that you see could use some strengthening. Be clear: *hitlamdut* is not an exercise in self-judgment but rather in self-knowledge. Only once you learn from your own experience the truth about the state of your inner life will you be in a position to cultivate the inner qualities that will ultimately lead you toward being more whole and more holy, all seven days of the week.

It is important to be on the lookout for what you can learn from the experiences that come your way, and that process is enhanced manyfold by keeping a journal. We are all so forgetful that even when we see something worth noting, that recognition is quickly swept away by the next set of experiences that come into our present moment. And those by the next.

When we add to that the fact that our human nature makes us want to forget, especially those experiences that we found to be uncomfortable or where we came up short of our expectations for ourselves—those experiences that might well contain the most important lessons we need to learn—then the introspection and reflection of a journaling practice become all the more important.

Journaling is a traditional Mussar practice.[1] It features in the nineteenth-century book *Cheshbon ha'Nefesh* by Rabbi Menachem Mendel Leffin. Later, every student in the Novarodok Mussar yeshivas in Europe carried a pocket-sized notebook in which they logged their daily experiences as they focused on cultivating character traits.

For the purposes of a Shabbat practice, you would journal on Saturday evening, focusing on your experiences during the day that had just concluded. Of course, you can write in the journal any day of the week, but it is your experiences on Shabbat that are most likely to contain the greatest lessons concerning the effect of that practice on your inner life, and so it is a priority to record those experiences on Saturday evening, when they are at their freshest.

Every chapter of this book focuses on a single inner trait that can be enriched through a Shabbat practice, and each of those chapters ends with suggestions of questions you can use to prompt your journaling.

Journaling gains maximum efficacy when the practice is done with consistency. Missing a day is no sin, but it is much better to write something, even very brief, rather than nothing at all, because when you write nothing, you break the chain of consistent engagement you are creating. This is a practice that pays off most when it becomes a habit.

Journaling fosters awareness in two ways. By reviewing the day that has just ended, you cast an eye over your experiences, and that review can make you more aware of things you actually overlooked in the hustle of the day or that you noted at the time but then promptly forgot. And once you get into the practice of journaling, just knowing that you will be facing your diary at the end of the day can cause you to sharpen your attention to events as they are happening to you.

You can write your notes with paper and pen, but if you prefer to keep an electronic journal, that is a fine option too. There are even a number of apps for journaling. How you do the practice is much less important than your commitment to doing it with consistency. If you develop consistency in keeping your journal, I guarantee that you will see a more remarkable Shabbat effect throughout your life.

Introduction

The drive to improve is deeply seated in the human soul, and every human being feels it. We intuit that we have the potential to be so much more than we are today. In the Jewish world, that impulse has given rise to a tradition of thought and practice called Mussar, which has been the focus of my study, writing, teaching, and personal practice for over twenty-five years.

Throughout the eleven centuries that the Mussar tradition has been developing,[1] it has kept one subject firmly in the spotlight: personal character. When you dig down into every success you have had in life, and equally into wherever you have come up short of your goals and your potential, you are sure to find that aspects of character played a fundamental role in whatever transpired.

The Mussar tradition contains priceless wisdom about your inner life and how to transform it, though the point is not to help you win friends and influence other people. The wise teachers of Mussar, drawing from the Torah and Jewish tradition, have insisted that all humans can and should aim much higher than that. The goals the Mussar teachers advise us to pursue are to be more whole and more holy. Or, in the words of Rabbi Yechezkel Levenstein (1895–1974), who was the Mussar guide of major yeshivas in Europe and Israel, "A person's primary mission in this world is to purify and elevate the soul."[2]

Because becoming more whole and more holy, or elevating the soul, can seem so impossibly lofty and far removed from our everyday concerns, the Mussar teachers through the centuries have encouraged us not to pay too much attention to those goals and to focus, instead, on the steps on the path that lead us toward them. The pathway of ascent they marked out directs us to take a careful look at our personal traits of character—what are known in Hebrew as *middot*—as they play out in everyday life, with an eye peeled especially for areas where we might still have as-yet unrealized potential.

Are you as generous as you know you could be? As enthusiastic in pursuing your goals? As compassionate? As kind? As strong? As truthful?

According to the Mussar teachers, working to develop our inner traits is the central activity of every aspect of our lives. Rabbi Yerucham Levovitz, an influential Mussar leader in Europe in the early twentieth century, illustrated this nicely by saying that if we ask a person who is baking matza what they are doing, the answer should not be, "I am baking matza," but rather, "I am developing the traits of watchfulness and alacrity."[3]

Accurately appraising your character and working to improve it is the Mussar pathway to personal spiritual growth. Rabbi Abraham Twerski says it very directly:[4]

To grow spiritually requires that we do two things: reinforce our positive character traits and reduce our negative character traits.

When you scrutinize your everyday experience, you are bound to find some traits of character in which you have the potential to do more and be better. Your efforts to develop those weaker qualities will move you closer to being the person you have the potential to be— ultimately, more whole and more holy.

Almost everything that exists in the Jewish world has roots in the Torah, and so you might well expect that directions for personal development would be found in that fundamental text of the Jewish world, but they are not. The Bible does not explicitly command us to be patient, disciplined, generous, kind, or compassionate. Thinkers in past generations have wondered why such important issues like these are not addressed in the Torah, and their answers fall into two categories.

One group sees the state of our character as the primary foundation for everything we do in our lives, including whether we will be successful in living up to our highest aspirations.

Rabbi Chaim Vital,[5] writing in the sixteenth century, notes that "character traits are not included in the 613 commandments of the Torah,"[6] and the reason for that, he says, is because they are "crucial preparations for the fulfillment or non-fulfillment of the commandments." In other words, the state of your character is what determines whether and how you will perform—or fail to perform—any goal-related task. That leads Rabbi Vital to conclude that "negative character traits are much worse than the sins [of breaching the commandments] themselves."

But, in the view of another group, character is not a prior foundation but rather an *outcome* of living a life guided by Torah principles. As long ago as the fifth century, in compilations of their teachings,[7] the rabbis noted what was at work here:

> The commandments were only given in order that people would be refined through them, because what does the Holy Blessed One care if one slaughters [an animal] from the front of the neck or if one slaughters from the back of the neck? We must say that the commandments were only given so that people would be refined through them.

The Hebrew word that is translated here as "refined" has the same linguistic root as the Hebrew word for "jeweler."[8] The notion of refinement the rabbis are pointing to has the same sense as in English: separating the valuable metal from the dross.

From this perspective, the biblical commandments to be charitable or to give tithes, for example, are not imposed to ensure that poor people are provided with the necessities of life, but rather they are meant to help people who are in a position to give overcome any tendency to be miserly and instead strengthen the trait of generosity.

Similarly, the Torah's prohibition against bearing grudges or seeking revenge is not to be seen as a mechanism meant to foster social harmony, but rather as a means to prevent an offended party from hardening their own heart through hatred and, instead, to reach for compassion and forgiveness.

In this book, I will draw mostly on the latter perspective and focus on the transformative impact that can come from living life according to biblical commandments, and in particular, the commandment to observe a weekly day of rest.

The fourth of the Ten Commandments directs:[9] "Remember the Sabbath, to keep it holy." What's involved in observing a weekly day of rest is expanded upon later in the same place:

> Six days you shall labor, and do all your work, but the seventh day is a Shabbat to the Lord your God. On it you shall not do any work, you, your son, your daughter, your male servant, your female servant, your livestock, and the sojourner who is within your gates. For in six days the Lord made heaven and earth, the sea, and all that is in them, and rested on the seventh day. Therefore, the Lord blessed the Sabbath day and made it holy.

It is hard to overstate just how revolutionary that command was in human history. It actually redefined human life. If every day of the week is given over to productive labor, then a human being is little more than an implement for material gain. But when work is limited to six days of the week, that makes room for something other than work to take a place in our lives. Six days a week a person is a laborer, and then the seventh day comes along and says, "You are more than just your labor. Who you are is more than just the sum of your productivity."

Over the centuries, biblical commentators have held up the practice of Shabbat[10] as a religious obligation, and in the contemporary world, in which our lives tend to be relentlessly hyper-busy, connected, frenetic, and anxious, caught up in an unabating torrent of technology, social media, and 24/7 work and home responsibilities, the notion of a day set aside for rest and delight has been extolled for the psychological, health, and social benefits it can bring.

This book takes a different approach. When God blessed the Sabbath and made it holy and then obligated us to sanctify and observe that special day, we were handed a unique opportunity to pursue our own spiritual elevation, our own sanctification, which is also an obligation presented to us in the Torah when it says, "You shall be holy."[11] It is my experience that observing a weekly day of rest can have a transformative impact on your personal nature as a human being.

~

I did not grow up with anything like a Sabbath in our household. My parents were Jews through and through, but they made the choice to be secular people, and the notion of rest on the Sabbath took the form of my father regularly napping on the couch while the announcer struggled to make the televised bowling match seem eventful.

I began observing my own Shabbat practice and brought it into our home only in mid-life, when I took a turn that brought me into direct engagement with my own Judaism. Shabbat became a regular part of my week only after I had begun to immerse myself in the study and practice of Mussar.

Mussar is a spiritual practice, and Shabbat at first glance seems to be a form of religious observance. Many people tend to plant their flag in one of these territories or the other, saying, "I'm spiritual but not religious," or "I'm a religious person; I don't have a spiritual bone in my body." In my experience, however, the two are not as separate as some people make them out to be. Spiritual practice without a formal structure (as religion provides) often proves to be flabby, undirected, and fleeting. And in the other direction, religion without spirituality can be rigid, with no beating heart.[12]

The person who seeks spiritual experiences that will take them soaring to ecstatic heights finds that they inevitably crash down to earth because they are just as human as the next person and, despite their spirituality, are still as prone to anger, envy, greed, and worry as anyone else. I remember years ago being in line to pick up mail at the American Express office in Kolkata, and at the next counter a young American, fully decked out with all the regalia of the Hare Krishna movement, including the saffron robes and the little pigtail at the back of his shaved skull, was yelling at the clerk: "I'm not angry. YOU are angry!!"

And the person who feels that their Shabbat practice is complete if they have ticked off all the many dos and don'ts specified in Jewish religious law has defaulted on the dividend that is the fruit of their practice. They emerge from Shabbat on Saturday evening satisfied that they observed Shabbat to a T, yet if they come out exactly the same person they were on Friday evening, with no trace of any movement whatsoever in their inner life, then their Shabbat has been hollow, and it is questionable whether it deserves to be called a Shabbat at all.

A Shabbat without a governing framework is no better than nodding off in front of the television for the sake of rest, while a Shabbat without spirit misses the point entirely. A Shabbat that is all about rest and relaxation has no more lasting impact than a beach vacation, while a day of rest that is a rote performance without concern for the spirit squeezes the life out of this rich and sacred day, reducing it to no more than a checklist of actions.

Shabbat is a locus where the lines of spirituality and religiosity are meant to cross, and not just cross, but to plait together to create a strong cord that will weave through all the days of your life. As such, this book can speak both to the person—whether Jewish or not—who, to date, has not engaged in a Shabbat practice, and just as well to the *shomer Shabbos* [Shabbat observant] person who endeavors to follow all the details of Jewish law as concerns Shabbat. And everyone in between.

～

Shabbat is called "a day of rest," but that can be misleading. The difference between a day of rest and a Shabbat practice lies in the fact that the latter requires that the day be "observed," which, in the traditional lexicon, means that one day in seven is structured and lived within frameworks that endorse and encourage certain types of activity and proscribe others. Within the Jewish world, these observances have been codified as a set of laws and practices that give shape and structure to the Sabbath day, some of them having to do with rest but dealing with other subjects as well. Many thick books have been written to detail the minutiae of Shabbat observance, and it is not my intention to contribute in any way to that cataloguing. Of course, I'll be touching on and exploring certain of these practices, but only as they are relevant to the specific focus we will pursue, which is to explore the impact taking a Shabbat practice can have on you and your life.

There is no single right way to observe Shabbat, and this book does not prescribe or endorse a particular format of practice. That's up to you. I was once a guest at a synagogue, and my host was one of the prayer leaders. As I stood beside him, a congregant came up, put his face right in my host's face, and for reasons known only to that person said challengingly, "I drove here today," which is something observant Jews do not do. My friend did not miss a beat and came back with, "What does that have to do with me? Your Shabbat observance is between you and God."

That is true, but still, we will be wise to pay close attention to the practices that have evolved within the Jewish world over the millennia, because every generation experimented and evaluated, and what has come down to us is collective wisdom about how to be successful in giving yourself the gift of an effective day of rest, one day in seven.

The central message of this book is that taking on a structured Shabbat practice with a spiritual core can bring about a transformation of a key set of inner traits, not just every seventh day, but with an effect that extends through every day of your life. Observing a Sabbath means carving out one day per week that you intentionally design and cause to be infused with awareness, joy, peace, rest, pleasure, holiness, and the like—qualities that, through practice and experience, get ingrained in you, and thus become characteristic of who you are in general.

That view of Shabbat and its impact has roots in the thought of the influential medieval commentator, Rashi,[13] who commented on the biblical verse "And the seventh day will be a day of complete rest,"[14] by explaining that what scripture is calling for is a "thorough rest" and not a "temporary rest."

Rabbi Chaim Shmuelevitz,[15] a leading Mussar teacher of the twentieth century, explains that a "temporary rest" means that a person tries to behave differently on Shabbat, but nothing penetrates deeply enough to actually change their character. They might bite their lips and force themselves not to express anger, for example, but inside, their heart is seething, and they will be just as prone to anger next week as they were last week. Or to take another example, they may not go into their office or follow the sports scores that day, but they are just as competitive on Shabbat in different ways, and no tempering of that trait takes place.

What the Torah means by a "complete rest," in contrast, is that a person transforms their character traits in a lasting way. Their efforts, which may have begun with the sort of restraint that defines a "temporary rest" on Shabbat, end up completely reworking the traits of anger and competitiveness at their root, in the heart.

It may seem ironic that we are being called to "work" on ourselves on a day of "rest." Even as we have our own inner reworking in mind, we need to remember the guidance of the prophet Isaiah (58:13), who said, "And you shall call the Sabbath a delight." The delights of a traditional day of rest, however, may not be immediately apparent to someone who has not experienced Shabbat. To them, Shabbat can appear to be a thicket of restrictions, since so many activities are proscribed from sunset Friday through sunset Saturday; shopping, driving, turning on the computer, cooking, making a phone call, gardening, and many more activities are avoided in order to create that day of rest. At first glance, it can seem that the "losses" must far outweigh the gains.

But anyone who has tasted the delight of Shabbat knows that cultivating and developing a Shabbat practice is not just a matter of staying away from the many activities that are not to be done on that day. Practicing Shabbat requires that we build up the inner strengths and capacities that make it possible to commit to and create a true day of peace and rest for ourselves. As we do that—as we develop the inner traits that are essential to opening up the Shabbat experience that is meant to enrich and refresh the soul—we actually reshape our inner life and gift ourselves with stronger inner traits [in Hebrew: *middot*] that take root in us and are then present in our lives all the other six days of the week as well.

I have to emphasize, however, that these impacts are not automatic. It is entirely possible for someone to observe a complete day of rest, replete with all the details, and yet it doesn't touch the soul or bring about significant change in their character. For Shabbat to induce the kind of transformation I am talking about and that I have seen in my own experience, it needs to be embraced with that as a conscious intention. From this perspective, a Shabbat practice is not just a religious obligation nor a refreshing breather from the pressures of daily life, but an investment in yourself and your own spiritual growth.

Here is an example to illustrate the sort of approach I have been describing and that will be explored in the chapters that follow.

One source for the word *shabbat* is the Hebrew root that means "to cease." Recall that the origin of Shabbat is God's act of creation of the world—on the seventh day, God ceased from all acts of creating and God rested. This is our model, and so when we observe Shabbat in our own lives, we also cease from our world-building activities.

In my experience, one of the most significant things people in our modern world can cease from doing in order to create a Shabbat experience is using their phones. There is a basis in Jewish law for shutting down the phone because it is a traditional Shabbat practice not to turn on or off any electrical device. But a day of unplugging has so much intrinsic appeal in our hyper-connected world that there are probably more contemporary books on the Sabbath written from Christian or self-help perspectives than there are Jewish.[16] It just makes sense: abundant studies and reports caution us that excessive time spent on screens and on social media can be damaging to the inner life, especially when the screen has become an addiction.[17]

Video game companies actually employ psychologists to design addiction into the game mechanisms. And recent reports have revealed that social media sites have also been deliberately designed to be addictive.[18] Many people find that to be true.

A Mussar student once asked for my advice on a problem he was facing. He and his family always hosted the extended family for a ritual Passover *seder* meal, and in recent years, his brother's family had been bringing their phones to the *seder* table. The result was that while the host was trying to lead the traditional ritual meal according to custom and to engage the table in discussion, his brother's children had their eyes focused just beneath the edge of the table, thumbs flying, texting, and who knows what else.

He wanted my advice, and I suggested that the best way to deal with the situation was to have a conversation with his brother well before the night of the *seder* to explain his hopes and aspirations for the family gathering, and to say that having the kids on their phones at the table was undermining the Passover experience for everyone. He should respectfully request that phones be turned off, or, better still, left at home for the sake of the family.

He followed my advice, had the conversation with his brother, and as a result, his brother's family has not attended a Passover *seder* since. Given the choice between a meaningful and engaged family gathering for a ritual meal and more screen time, they opted for the screen.

Because screentime can be just that addictive, people can find it very difficult to shut down their devices, no easier than breaking any other form of addiction. Even in the Orthodox synagogue I attend, it is not unusual for a phone in someone's pocket to ring during Shabbat services. But if we are truly committed to experiencing a spiritual day, a day of peace, joy, rest, and delight in our week, then we have no choice but to press pause on the relentless assault the media wages on our minds, hearts, emotions, and souls through devices. As long as the phone, the tablet, or the laptop is allowed uncontrolled access to our lives, peace, joy, and rest are simply unattainable.

What drives us to the phone is the desire to communicate, the desire to have instant access to information, the desire to be seen, and the desire to be included in the conversation. Pressing the "off" button becomes possible for us only when we gain mastery over those desires. Taking on our desires and establishing some mastery over them makes Shabbat possible. Once we actually do succeed in that difficult task; however, we will find that we have gifted ourselves with a new strength that is available for us to call on all the days of our life, where many sorts of desires may be driving our behavior, including in ways that are clearly negative.

By turning off the phone one day every week, we provide ourselves with living proof that we are able to rule over our desires rather than having them control us. Making a practice of shutting down from Friday evening until Saturday night actually demonstrates to ourselves that we have the capacity to turn off the phone at any time we choose. Even more generally, getting good at clicking "off" strengthens the will and demonstrates to us that we have the power to decide what to participate in and what to ignore, and to limit what we engage in to the things and the extent that we freely choose, without compulsion.

Now having explored this example of how shutting down is a Shabbat practice that has an impact all week long, I want to make clear that the choice whether to undertake any practice discussed in this book is freely yours to make. The starting point for our exploration is not a requirement that you turn off your phone or take on any other stipulated practices. The goal is to explore in order that you will understand and appreciate how such practices work—both for creating a holy day of rest *and* for influencing our lives throughout the week. What you do with that information is entirely up to you or, as my friend said, it's between you and God.

The material for this book was initially developed for a course I offered within The Mussar Institute, in the first instance in collaboration with Rabbi Micha Berger, and afterward on my own. I am grateful to the many students in those courses whose feedback and experiences helped to hone and refine these teachings. Their positive response to the course inspired me to make these teachings more widely available.

As an example, one student reflected on the impact his day of rest practice has had on his entire life:

> Shabbat practice caused me to get better at pausing in all kinds of contexts, dwelling in the hiatus of being there instead of pushing forward (which I can do obsessively). In that pause I listen to whomever I meet and also find enjoyment in what's being said; letting tasks take their shifts and slips without getting frustrated. I find a fuller sense of general purpose—that is, a sense of meaning that transcends whatever I'm focused on.

I have observed that there are eight personal traits that are essential to observing Shabbat. These, in turn, are strengthened and enhanced by Shabbat observance. The practices of a day of rest thus become vehicles for fostering these traits, and, once cultivated, these fortified traits show up in new ways that transform everyday life.

We'll start with the character trait called *zehirut* in Hebrew, which can be translated into English as "awareness."[19] It takes keen awareness to maintain the boundaries that are integral to a Shabbat practice, and when you practice paying attention to the lines and limits that turn the day away from labor and toward rest, you will find that you have sharpened your sense of awareness in a lasting and pervasive way that can apply in many contexts.

We'll then proceed to explore seven other traits that get developed through a Shabbat practice:

- Holiness
- Contentment
- Joy
- Rest
- Peace
- Silence
- Trust

There could be more as well, but in my experience, these eight are central both to Shabbat practice and to helping you become the more whole and holy person you have the potential to be.

To assist you in developing these qualities and making that transition, every chapter provides not only insights and principles but also helpful practices for developing the trait in focus in that chapter, including maintaining a journal to track your progress and build your awareness. Journaling is a traditional Mussar method that enhances awareness and deepens the impact of the practice.

~

The traditional greeting for the Sabbath is "Shabbat Shalom," which is generally translated as a wish for a "peaceful Sabbath." But the Hebrew word "*shalom*" that translates as "peace" comes from a linguistic root that means "whole." Our workaday lives can be so scattered and fragmented, sometimes even broken, that the only way we can savor the sweet taste of a life characterized by wholeness, with nothing lacking, is by fostering that experience, and that is precisely what Shabbat is all about. The dividend is peace.

My hope is that this book will help you to experience a more whole and peaceful you, at first once every seven days, and then, through that practice, to experience a life infused with peace, joy, rest, trust, and other wonderful human qualities that are available to you if you make the effort to acquire them.

1

Awareness

The Watchful Mind

In every aspect of our lives, there are boundaries we draw or that are drawn for us, and sometimes the penalty for crossing them can be severe. What does it take to be sharply aware of the boundaries we want to observe and respect in our behavior? We might say it takes caution, or watchfulness, or even, vigilance. It turns out that these are all English words used to translate the Hebrew term *zehirut*.[1] That's the word that shows up on road signs in Israel when you are driving along and you come to a dangerous intersection. The yellow sign by the roadside will warn you "*zehirut*," which means "be careful."

But there is a deeper meaning of the term revealed in the fact that the word derives from a Hebrew source that signifies something quite different from "caution." The word *zehirut*[2] shares a linguistic root with other words that have the meaning of "shining." It's that same root that gives rise to the title of the celebrated book of Jewish mysticism called the *Zohar*, which translates as "Radiance." A related word is used in the prayer book and in the Torah to describe the shining of the sun.[3]

The two notions of "caution" and "shining" might seem at first glance to have nothing to do with one another, but they are not as disconnected as they appear. What links them is the recognition that the ability to act with caution depends on having an alert—one could say, *shining*—mind. Only when consciousness is brightly illuminated will we be in a position to be vigilant about our actions rather than governed by our habits or unconscious forces.

Unfortunately for us, many of the things we do in our everyday lives can have the effect of dulling the brightness of consciousness. I suspect you may know your own version of the experience and are familiar with some of its causes.

When the mind is dull, the world appears as if seen through a shadowy veil, or as if the light has been dimmed to a low level. Sometimes this dull mind is called "foggy," and that describes the experience well.

A fog descends and the world is encountered through a blurring haze. In that state, people are not fully aware of time or their surroundings or the people around them, and they find it difficult to pay attention. When we are in the grip of a dull mind, we have car accidents, we miscommunicate in emails, we stumble over things, we don't hear what people are saying, and we fumble.

What causes the mind to turn dull? For a few people, that would be an inherent condition, or maybe it is the outcome of illness, or a side effect of taking drugs to deal with an illness. But besides people suffering from conditions like those, the rest of us tend to feel dull when we are exhausted from working long hours, or with unrelieved mental exertion. Lack of sleep, certain foods, too much screen time . . . you might well be very familiar from your own experience with what causes your mind to fog over.

In the eighteenth-century Mussar classic, *Path of the Just*, Rabbi Moshe Chaim Luzzatto singles out three factors that he says tend to get in the way of the bright consciousness of *zehirut*. He lists:

- Being engrossed in worldly affairs that so preoccupy a person that the outer world fades away;

- Excessive laughter and mockery that, in his words, "destroy a person's heart until reason and knowledge no longer rule. One becomes like a drunkard or a mad person"; and

- Bad company.

I think we have to include in this last category a type of person that did not exist in Rabbi Luzzatto's time, which includes digital companions, like news commentators, social influencers, politicians, characters from movies and television, and the like, who deliberately set out to fill our minds with preoccupying anxieties and ideas and, in so doing, induce dullness.

And we know from experience that the list doesn't stop there. You can and should look at your own experience and behavior to see what it is that has the effect of dulling your own mind. You quite possibly already know.

Contrast the dull mind with the radiant mind. The bright mind sees clearly, with a quality like we experience when we awaken to look out over the desert on a crisp winter morning. Everything is illuminated in sharp outline, with vivid colors, and your awareness is attentive to anything that stirs or moves.

The sage who pointed out that the word *zehirut* derives from the root meaning of "shining" was Rabbi David ben Maimon, who lived from 1222 to 1300 CE. He served as the leader of Egyptian Jewry and was the grandson of the famous sage Maimonides, the Rambam. The illuminated quality of mind, he said,[4] comes to us because:

1. we think enlightening thoughts,

2. we tap into the light of divine luminescence that infuses reality, or

3. we experience intellectual flashes of the spirit.

I have no argument with those three points. But, in reality, I see the shining mind a little more prosaically and hence as a more common phenomenon that is available to all of us more of the time.

In my own understanding and experience, the bright mind is actually an innate faculty of a healthy and functional human being— as long as that mind is not being dulled in any way. Rather than an elevated, mystical state of illumination, it is really the default reality that is available to any ordinary human being when we stop soiling our minds and, instead, polish them through our choices and actions.

We have reviewed some of the things that dull the mind, and what I see from my own experience is that when I stop doing those things to myself—and when I am blessed with a good night's sleep— what emerges is a mental faculty that is more fully awake to what is happening all around, less subject to distraction, and that has insight into the connections and the meaning of what I am perceiving.

The quality of mind we are discussing is not just something excavated from Jewish teachings in thirteenth-century Egypt. We can find that understanding reflected in the contemporary psychological literature as well.

What I am calling a bright mind is referred to in psychology as "wakefulness." In the introduction to his classic in the field, called *Sleep and Wakefulness*, Nathaniel Kleitman explains the term wakefulness by invoking synonyms such as alertness, watchfulness, attentiveness, and awakeness. It's interesting that "watchfulness" shows up on this list because that is one of the standard translations of the Hebrew term *zehirut*. These terms constitute what he calls "a state of being wide-awake," exactly what we are talking about as well.

Scientific research associates wakefulness with the cognitive ability to encode new experiences into memory and systematically retrieve past experiences, respond to and interact with the environment, and exhibit a wide variety of problem-solving abilities. All these capacities are dependent on the light of consciousness shining brightly.

This brings us to the big question and our special focus: How is having a wakeful consciousness relevant to the Shabbat experience? And how is Shabbat—which is so often marked by a glass of wine, a big meal, and a delicious afternoon nap—relevant to the mental quality of *zehirut*?

Shabbat Mind

The word for character traits in Hebrew is *middot*, and when I first discovered that there is an entire book of Jewish law (i.e., the Mishnah[5]) called "*Middot*," I was excited to find out what the rabbis writing almost 2,000 years ago had to say about human nature. I was shocked and disappointed to discover that the four chapters of tractate *Middot* are entirely given over to documenting the measurements of the Temple compound that historically stood in Jerusalem.

What I did learn is that the Temple courtyard on the mount measured 135 cubits from north to south and 187 cubits from east to west and was surrounded by walls, but absolutely nothing about human character.

Turns out that the word *middot* literally means "measures" and can be applied as much to measuring the dimensions of an object as it can to taking the "measure" of a human being.

Although it wasn't what I was looking for, I was nevertheless fascinated by the precision the rabbis brought to their measurements of the temple. For example:

The Rampart [within the Temple Mount] was ten cubits broad. And there were twelve steps there; the height of each step was half a cubit, and the tread thereof was half a cubit. All the steps were at the height of half a cubit and the tread thereof was half a cubit, save only those of the Porch. All the entrances and gates that were there were twenty cubits high and ten cubits wide, save only those of the Porch.

The temple was measured in such detail because this structure was, in its time, the uncontested central focus of Jewish life. But history taught a harsh lesson—not once, but twice—that any physical location is vulnerable to being lost or destroyed, as happened to both the first and second Temples.

The destruction of the Second Temple in 70 CE brought about a shift in focus in Jewish ideas about holiness. The primary locus of the sacred moved away from the realm of space and toward the sanctification of time. Unlike a physical building or a holy mountain, a sacred day is completely portable and can be carried and observed anywhere that people happen to find themselves. This suited the needs of the Jewish people in the long centuries of exile.

Shabbat became a temple carved out of time, and the same precision that was devoted to measuring the length and breadth of the physical Temple came to be applied to the observance of Shabbat.

Every week, the Sabbath begins at the moment the sun sinks below the horizon on Friday evening. When the rituals of Shabbat were first developed, there were no charts or graphs that could be relied on to tell the community when that exact moment actually arrived, and all it took was a cloudy day to make the time of sunset unknowable. That led the rabbis to institute a rule that we should begin Shabbat observance eighteen minutes before the sun sets in order not risk crossing the line of sunset. Nowadays, even though we know with precision the time of sunset, those eighteen minutes provide a buffer period just to ensure that no delay will cause us to miss bringing in Shabbat before the sun sets.

These rules make the timing for Shabbat both specific and variable. Candles are lit to initiate the holy day precisely eighteen minutes before sunset, but in the winter, that might take place at 4 p.m., whereas in the summer, candles might be lit at 9 p.m. or even later. The exact time also varies depending on your geographical location. You have to be alert to know the time for beginning Shabbat because it changes every week, as the earth moves through the cycle of the seasons of the year and the days lengthen and shorten accordingly.

The same sort of issue of timing also applies to the other end of Shabbat, the time on Saturday evening when it finishes.

This concern for exact timing reflects a broader principle that shows up throughout Shabbat observance, which is that a structure with boundaries is extremely helpful and, for most of us, essential if we hope to achieve a spiritual day of rest. A web of precise lines we are meant to heed and not cross establishes the boundaries that distinguish and separate the holy from the mundane, thus serve to establish and protect the sanctity of the seventh day.

The lines regarding timing are drawn with precision, and there are also categories of things that are set aside and not to be touched on Shabbat: computer, stove, phone, lights, television, car, and the list goes on. This is actually a single category of things that are turned on or off from a source of power that became taboo on Shabbat once the biblical prohibition on lighting or extinguishing a fire[6] got extended to any kind of use of power, including electricity.[7]

On any day of the work week, we pick up the phone or switch off a light without a second thought. The ease with which we do those sorts of things can make it challenging to observe Shabbat and its strictures because only on that day do we restrict activities that are fully permissible the other six days of the week. Those boundaries serve to protect the unique holiness of the day, but because those limits don't even exist for us on the other days of the week, on Shabbat we need to be sharply aware of lines that are of no concern on the other days of the week.

Most of the time, we tend to operate from habit, and it doesn't matter much if we are a bit sloppy in how we conduct our ordinary everyday activities. That is not the case on Shabbat, when our intention is to build a temple in time. A holy day of rest needs to be very different from the other six days of the week, and establishing and protecting that holiness and our experience of it requires that we shake loose from our habits and instead operate with full alertness to what we are doing, or about to do, so that we won't cross any lines that would not even exist for us on ordinary days.

When the Torah tells us to observe Shabbat, in the two places where that commandment is given, two different verbs are used: "*zakhor*" [remember][8] and "*shamor*" [guard][9] "the Shabbat day to keep it holy." Both acts we are called to perform in order to sanctify Shabbat—remembering and guarding—require us to be conscious and present in our attention to the day at hand.

This requirement to have a bright awareness applies especially to the many discernments and boundaries that are built into Shabbat observance. In no fewer than twelve places, the Torah reiterates the prohibition against doing work on Shabbat, but nowhere does Scripture define "work." The rabbis who compiled the Talmud applied themselves to defining the restrictions in this area and identified thirty-nine core activities that are forbidden on Shabbat.[10] Their list derives from the fact that the Torah mentions the activity of building the Tabernacle right alongside the commandment to observe Shabbat, and so the sages deduced that the thirty-nine types of work that were employed to construct and operate the Tabernacle constitute a set of things we are to avoid doing on Shabbat.

For example, the first types of labor that are marked as prohibited are collectively referred to as "*sidurah d'pat*," which means "the order of bread." Showbreads were on display in the Tabernacle, and making them required planting, plowing, harvesting, threshing, grinding, sifting, kneading, etc.—a total of eleven types of activity. Since that is what they did in the Tabernacle, those bread-producing activities are all considered forbidden activities on Shabbat.

You might be a baker, and then one of the circumscribed activities is directly relevant to you, but as for the others, very few of us plant, plow, harvest, thresh, grind, and so on. It may seem at first glance that these areas of activity are therefore totally irrelevant to the majority of us, but it is actually not so. These agricultural categories derive from the bread production process, but they define general types of activities that show up elsewhere as well.

Planting wheat to make bread is proscribed, and that leads to the prohibition against all planting, which makes it inappropriate to tend to your household garden on Shabbat.

And to give another example, since the wheat was ground, grinding is defined as a prohibited activity. You may not make it a practice to grind your own flour, but could there be instances in your own activities where you might do some grinding? Can I offer you a little pepper for the soup?

In the space that exists between the desire to add some pepper to your food and your hand reaching out to take hold of the container that holds the pepper lives the possibility of *zehirut*, being brightly aware, and in that illumination to discern whether the pepper you are reaching for is to be found in a shaker or a mill. Shaking pre-ground pepper is an entirely different—and permitted—activity compared to grinding pepper in a peppermill, which is prohibited.

Here is another example. Let's imagine that you are out for a walk on the city street and you have the impulse to pluck a leaf from a bush, or pick a flower, or to weed a dandelion from your lawn. Activities like that are easily done in modern city living, and they happen to be included in the eleven types of labor that go into making bread under the category of *kotzer*, which means "harvesting."

Will it change the world, or earn you a front row seat in the underworld, if you grind pepper, or pick a flower on Shabbat? The act itself is not the point, just as nothing of real consequence happens when the golf ball drops into the hole, or the basketball swishes through the hoop. Our focus is not meant to emphasize the peppermill but the hand that holds it, and especially the mind of the person who directs that hand.

So, let's say you are committed to the practice of not engaging in acts of harvesting on Shabbat. Now imagine you are walking along the street and you run into a friend. You stop to chat, and while you are engrossed in the interesting conversation with someone you have not seen for a while, your hand absent-mindedly reaches out first to stroke an inviting leaf on a bush by the sidewalk, and then, without even being aware of how it happened, you find that you are holding the leaf between two of your fingers. On a weekday, you could do that, no problem, but this is happening on Shabbat when there is a prohibition on harvesting.

The leaf got plucked simply because of a dull mind. Only later do you realize, "Oh my God, I picked the leaf!"

Contrast that with what happens in a brightly aware mind, where the impulse stands out to be evaluated in the clear light of consciousness, where it is recognized in advance as a potential breach of a commitment, and the hand is directed to withdraw.

Zehirut is what a person calls on when he or she wants to act with conscious intent and not just according to unconscious impulse. It is the quality of mind that makes it possible for us to stop to consider the choice of whether to act in a certain way, or perhaps not at all, as well as the motivations that are instigating the desire to act, and the ideals we want to bring into our action at that time.

Or to give another example, let's say you follow the rule of not turning on or off lights on Shabbat. Many people who follow that practice leave the bathroom light on for the duration of Shabbat. At some point, you go to the bathroom, finish washing your hands, and as you are heading out the door, out of sheer habit, you reach out to turn off the light switch. What then? Whether you actually do or do not flip the switch is determined by the quality of *zehirut* you have developed.

The key question to ask yourself here is whether you are content to have your actions governed by habit, or do you see it as preferable to have conscious choice guide your hand? The fact is that we can get into a lot of trouble when we act on unconscious and unexamined impulses. How many times have I regretted something done without conscious intent, because I did not open up the space between the impulse and the action, or what my late Mussar teacher, Rabbi Yechiel Yitzchok Perr, once called "the space between the match and the fuse"?

Eating foods we know we should not be eating, allowing ourselves to interact with people who are not good influences, stealing things, and blurting out gossip are among the innumerable examples of actions we can allow to happen—not as a result of conscious choice but as an outcome of unexamined impulse or habit. And these sorts of behavior do have major consequences.

Remembering and guarding boundaries on Shabbat is not the only way we can cultivate *zehirut* on that holy day. There is also the issue of the mindfulness we bring to activities that are actually permitted to us. We are enjoined to eat and drink and enjoy ourselves on Shabbat, but we need attentiveness to ensure that when we do something that is permitted, or even required (like saying blessings), we do those things in the full light of a well-illuminated mind.

Our guide in "caution in regard to permitted activities" is the Ramban, Rabbi Moses ben Nachman, often called Nachmanides, a thirteenth-century Sephardic rabbi, and biblical commentator. Ramban points out that the Torah permits certain things, like drinking wine, eating meat, and having intimacy in marital life, but it sets no limits on those activities. Therefore, it falls to us to rein ourselves in so we do not drink ourselves into a stupor, eat meat like a glutton, or pursue physical pleasure like an obsession (or, in the colorful language of the rabbis, like a rooster).

Our wise ancestors who developed the practices of Shabbat understood that there was a quality of mind that was essential to observing Shabbat. They also appreciated that observing Shabbat could play a powerful role in helping us to develop that awareness and that it would be of service to us the other six days of the week as well.

We find that to be the message in the Talmudic tractate that deals with Shabbat, which talks at length about the liability a person faces for transgressing one of the forbidden labors due to a lapse of mental awareness. In ancient Israel, when the Temple stood, if you inadvertently engaged in an act of planting or plowing or harvesting, or the like, on Shabbat, you atoned for that misstep by bringing a specific type of animal sacrifice[11] to the Temple.

The term that is used to describe this lapse in awareness that led to the inadvertent transgression is *he'elam*, a word that comes from the linguistic root that means "to disappear" or "to vanish."

When your mind is in a state of dullness, it is as if you have disappeared. In truth, we should not say that dullness is "as if" you have disappeared because it is actually the reality. When your consciousness is dull, the "you" who shows up in your conscious mind is simply not there anymore. You have effectively vanished.

Polishing the Mirror of the Mind

Zehirut is an important and desirable inner trait because it gives you the ability to act from conscious intent rather than out of dullness, instinct, habit, or in response to the demands of desire. Heeding the boundaries that our rabbis have instituted for Shabbat requires that we be very present and alert in the moment because, in the blink of an eye, a lapse in awareness can lead to crossing a line. In the moment when we are not brightly alert, the pepper gets ground, the leaf gets picked, the light gets turned off, and the phone gets checked.

From this perspective, engaging with Shabbat, and in particular with the restrictions built into Shabbat observance, does not appear as an austerity or a deprivation but as an effective aid to developing the capacity to be brightly alert at all times. When we train ourselves to be the kind of people who are capable of catching ourselves before we act, we build up the power of *zehirut*. Having a set of boundaries we practice not crossing is an excellent method for doing just that. The *zehirut* we cultivate through Shabbat observance will then be implanted within us, ready to serve us in every context of our lives.

Following the lines we have just explored, I want to suggest a practice to cultivate *zehirut*. You can put this practice "in your pocket," ready for any situation that happens to arise on Shabbat that has the potential to trigger you in some way, whether in anger or temptation or envy or whatever tends to stimulate a response that leads you to stray where you would not choose to go.

This practice breaks down into three parts that apply to any area where you have determined to set a line on your behavior. It could be not checking your phone, not turning on the coffee machine, driving the car, shopping, or something else.

Even if you already have a full-fledged Shabbat practice, that observance can become so comfortable and habitual that it makes no contribution to developing more bright-mindedness. In that case, you might choose to draw a line on engaging in something perhaps more subtle, like paying attention to the news of the day or entering conversations about everyday life. Or you might choose to do things slower than your natural pace.

Whatever line you have set for yourself, when you feel that you are drawing close to crossing it, be ready to do the following:

a. Catch hold of the feeling that is triggering you to take action before you react to it.

b. Hold that feeling in abeyance, consider both what is motivating you to act on the feeling as well as what it is that might move you to resist the impulse. A simple example to illustrate: you crave the piece of cake, but at the same time, you know it is not on your diet.

c. Reinforce to yourself what you had committed to yourself would be the line you would not cross, and strengthen your will to adhere to your chosen response.

Review the steps in this process several times so they are firmly in your mind in preparation for Shabbat.

The essential aspect of the practice is that it opens up a space of time between a stimulus and response, or a space "between the match and the fuse," as Rabbi Perr put it. In that space, you have the possibility of acting with your free will, according to your own goals and commitments.

Once you are clear on the three-step process, you can apply it in relation to something you determine in advance that you do not want to do. A variation on the practice is to apply it in an area where you have no restriction on the activity, but you have set a limit on the extent of your participation in that permitted activity.

What gives added impact to the experiences that derive from doing these practices is journaling about them in the evening, after Shabbat has ended.

To guide your journaling, write out the intention you set out to observe, and then ask yourself questions like:

- Did you do what you set out to do?

- Was it easy or difficult for you?

- What challenges or obstacles did you encounter?

- What unexpected sources of strength or awareness showed up?

- What lessons did you learn?

Even as you journal, keep in touch with the quality of mind you are bringing to the task, whether dull, or bright or somewhere in between. After all, the quality of consciousness that we have had in focus here is meant to be strengthened for the sake of every activity, every day of the week.

2

Rest

Rested and Refreshed

Ah, rest! We are all so busy, so tugged this way and that, so torn by commitments, so anxious with worries, so exhausted so much of the time, and seemingly always falling farther and farther behind. What a sweet delight to think of giving ourselves the gift of rest.

Let's be very clear that the kind of rest that concerns us here should not be mistaken for mindless, blobbing-out. When the Torah reports that on the first day of creation, God created both light and dark, it is telling us that darkness is not just the absence of light but a created reality of its own. The same is true of rest (in Hebrew: *menucha*). Rest is not just the absence of work. It is an actual reality in itself.

That message comes through in the verses that tell us about Shabbat. Genesis 2:2 reads:

On the seventh day God completed the work that God had done, and God abstained on the seventh day from all the work that God had done.

The first part of the verse tells us that creation was not complete until the seventh day, which implies that God actually did something on the seventh day to complete creation. Yet the end of the verse says that God abstained from work on the seventh day, implying that no work at all was performed then. What could God have done on that first Shabbat that satisfies both of these implications? According to the medieval commentator Rashi, on the seventh day God created the last thing the world needed for it to be complete. "What did the world lack?" he asks. And he answers: "Rest. When Shabbat came, rest came, and then the work of creation was finished and completed."

Rest is more than just the *absence* of labor. I can steer away from doing any kind of work, like building or demolishing, cooking, driving, or making, but does that guarantee that I will be in a state of repose? It does not. I might find myself agitated and upset about any or all of the things I am not dealing with. And further, it is entirely possible to avoid doing any kind of labor and still be as busy and frantic as ever with thoughts and speech!

This is Rashi's message: rest is a creation in its own right. If we want to rest, then we need to set down the pen or the plow or the keyboard and withdraw from laborious, world-building activities, and then we need to go another step to embrace and immerse ourselves in rest itself.

Rabbi Eliyahu Dessler, the great Mussar teacher of the mid-twentieth century, makes an important point in this context. He clarifies that "*menucha* does not refer to laziness, which is in reality a form of destructiveness and death." The essence of *menucha*, he says, is that it affords us "a break from material, physical existence. It is a spiritual restfulness and peace."[1]

This is helpful because, as we will soon see, it relocates the definition of *menucha* from outward actions to inner states of being—not just what we do, but also our inner state when we do it.

Resting on Shabbat

Rabbi Dessler's distinction helps us make sense of the fact that a person can do a lot of what appears to be labor on Shabbat: laying out food, cleaning up after the meal, serving guests. That is not a contradiction as long as we understand that the kind of rest that earns the name *menucha* is defined by our inner spiritual aspiration as we dedicate it to the higher goals we are pursuing.

Rabbi Mordechai Becher[2] tells the story of spending a Shabbat in Hong Kong where he was assigned a room on the ninth floor of his hotel. As a Shabbat-observant Jew, Rabbi Becher did not use the elevator on Shabbat and instead hiked up and down the stairs, which were, by rule, restricted for use by the hotel staff.

When one of the staff encountered Rabbi Becher huffing and puffing up the stairs, she asked, "Sir, why don't you use the elevator?" Through his breathlessness, Rabbi Becher managed to respond, "It is my day of rest."

The literal meaning of the word *"shabbat"* is "stop" or "cease," but that does not mean that on Shabbat, we become inert. Rather, we call a halt to our striving to build our world. Modeling our behavior on God who rested on the seventh day of creation, on our own Shabbat we forgo the ordinary world and all its mundane concerns, along with our own frantic efforts to get things done (and then do more). On Shabbat, we set down what is burdening us. We cease to create. We bring the spirit to rest.

Rest is the quality that lies right at the heart of Shabbat, since the primary commandment we are given for the seventh day is the requirement to rest.[3] The Torah says it clearly (Exodus 20:9-10):

Six days you shall labor and do all your work, but the seventh day is a Sabbath to the Lord your God; you shall not do any work, neither you, nor your son or daughter, nor your male or female servant, nor your animals, nor any foreigner residing in your towns.[4]

The Torah puts so much emphasis on resting on Shabbat that it instructs us that even slaves and draft animals are to cease from working on that day, even during the critical plowing and harvest seasons. The upshot in our world would be that it is a violation of the spirit of resting on Shabbat if, on Saturday morning, you send your dog to retrieve the newspaper from the front porch. It's her day of rest as well!

In another place, the Torah explains the reason to rest. It provides a positive directive telling us to embrace rest on Shabbat in order that our weary bodies and souls can be refreshed:

> Six days do your work, but on the seventh day do not work, so that your ox and your donkey may rest, and so that the slave born in your household and the foreigner living among you may be refreshed.[5]

The word translated as "refreshed" in the last quote from the Bible is *v'yinafash*. It's an interesting word that shows up tellingly in an earlier place in the Bible as well. When we look at the biblical verse that says that God ceased to create on the seventh day (Exodus 31:17), that same word recurs:

> And on the seventh day, God ceased from work and was "*yinafash*."

In that context, the word is almost always translated as "rested." That's curious. We learned that the word *v'yinafash* means to be refreshed, and we have to wonder, did God need to be "refreshed"? Did God put out so much energy in the first six days that God was nearing exhaustion and needed a break in order to get back to full strength, so to speak?

That can't be, of course, so there must be another way to translate *v'yinafash*. In the biblical concordance,[6] we do find the definition of "be refreshed," and then the term is explained as coming from a root that means "to breathe." That reference to breathing shows up in another word from the same root, which is *nefesh*, meaning "soul." A soul is present only so long as the being is breathing.

Rashi speaks directly to this issue. In his comments on the verse in which God was "refreshed," he says:

> Every expression of *nofesh* [rest], is an expression of *nefesh* [soul], for one regains one's soul and one's breath when one rests from the toil of work. God, about Whom it is written, "God neither tires nor wearies" (Isaiah 40:28), and Whose every act is performed by speech [i.e., without physical effort], dictated rest in reference to God's-self [only] in order *to make it understood to the [human] ear* with words that it can understand.

Drawing together those two dimensions of the word *v'yinafash*—breath and soul—gives us a basis for saying that on the seventh day of creation, God took a soulful breath. God did that not because the work of creation had been so grueling that God needed to take a day off, but to establish a model that we, who are prone to exhaustion, can follow on our own seventh day: on Shabbat, we need to set down our burdens and savor a soulful breath in order to be refreshed.

That soulful breath is predicated on our having first ceased from any activities that are intended to create something that does not already exist. Just as God completed the productive labor of forming the universe in six days, so should we content ourselves with what we can get done during the six days of productivity that are allocated to every week.

Then, on Shabbat, we create rest for ourselves. This rest stands as resistance to the idea that a person is nothing but an engine of production. It disrupts the compulsion to do more that grips most of our lives. It disputes the sense that eats at us, that we are never doing enough. By embracing and enforcing rest, we replace those ideas with the conviction that who we are, right now, is truly enough.

A Restful Soul

We can't possibly come to rest until we have ceased from working. That brings the body to rest. But that is only a necessary preparation. We still need to go on to create the conditions that bring the soul to rest. As we saw, *v'yinafash* is a soulful rest because it embodies the Hebrew word for "soul" [*nefesh*]. It is related to a quality the rabbis speak of, labeled *menuchat ha'nefesh*, a term that translates into English as "calmness of the soul" and points us to the quality of inner rest we might better call "equanimity."

We position ourselves to be able to rest, breathe, and refresh by taking on the prohibition, "Do no productive work." That causes us to step back from all the creative activities of life that we busy ourselves with for six days. But on its own, ceasing work will not give us the rest we seek. To that negative directive, we need to add a positive pathway: "Cultivate a calm soul," which means stepping into an inner state of equanimity.

A calm soul is an alluring possibility. We are often so agitated, worried, and upset that we barely perceive what is actually happening in and around us. Have you ever eaten a meal in such a state of agitation that you have no recollection of what it was you ate? It is possible to get through an entire meal and not taste a single bite. This can't be the ideal for the soul.

But neither is a detached state of numbness the goal. The Jewish view of equanimity does not call on us to detach into a feelingless, flat-lined, emotional coma. That message is conveyed clearly by Rabbi Adin Steinsalz:[7]

> The Jewish approach to life considers the man who has stopped going—he who has a feeling of completion, of peace, of a great light from above that has brought him to rest—to be someone who has lost his way. Only he whom the light continues to beckon, for whom the light is as distant as ever, only he can be considered to have received some sort of response.

But neither is it ideal to be tossed around like a cork on the ocean waves. We get a great image of what ideal equanimity looks like from the fact that the linguistic root that gives rise to the word *menucha*, which is our subject here, also shows up in the name of the shipbuilder made famous by his Ark and the biblical two-by-two story. The soul can be likened to Noah's[8] ark because our experience of living in the jostling, uncertain world is very akin to being tossed about on the waves of the sea. Equanimity is the inner quality of being like Noah, who holds steady amid the storms of life and does not capsize.

When the Torah describes the end of the flood, it employs various forms of the word "*menucha*." For example, when the floodwaters begin to recede and the ark lodges on the mountain, it is described as "*vatanch ha'teivah*"—the ark came to rest.

In that case, however, it is the rest that came after the (literal!) storm. The challenge in Mussar practice is to achieve *menucha* even as the storm rages around us. Rabbi Yosef Yozel Hurwitz, the Mussar teacher who became known as the Alter of Novardok, makes this point by distinguishing between *menucha* and another Hebrew word, *shalva*.[9] He sees a state of *shalva* as the restful frame of mind of a person who does not have any problems. *Menucha*, in contrast, is an inner state that permits a person to face their life challenges with a restful mind. The problems are very real, but they do not upset the person's inner equilibrium.

Shabbat is a laboratory in which to practice and develop the capacity for equanimity. That's the point of a story that was often told by Rabbi Yerucham Levovitz, who was the Mussar supervisor of the Mir yeshiva in Europe in the early twentieth century. The daughter of Rav Yerucham's teacher[10] was very ill and was visited by a prominent physician who told her that what she needed to do to be cured of her illness was to attain equanimity, not to get upset or angry.

The daughter related to her father what the doctor had said, and he responded that she should have asked the doctor how one attains equanimity. "You should have asked him: what is the diet for *menuchat ha'nefesh*?"

After quoting this incident, Rav Yerucham himself answered the question. He said that the diet that produces a calm inner being is Shabbat, in all its splendid detail. In his words, Shabbat is "a complete diet for attaining equanimity."[11]

How so? Well, many commentators say that a dominant characteristic of Shabbat is *perfection*. On Shabbat, we have no need to do any sort of constructive activity involving human intelligence, strength, or skill because the world is already perfect just the way it is. We don't labor on Shabbat because, in a perfect world, there is simply nothing that needs doing.

Shabbat is the seventh day, and in Jewish thought, seven is the number that represents completeness and wholeness. Besides Shabbat being the seventh day, we have the sabbatical year for the land in the seventh year of a seven-year cycle, and the jubilee,[12] as the culmination of seven cycles of seven years.

When we embrace the day as perfect just the way it is, it becomes possible for us to experience peace of mind. Don't think our rabbis were so naïve or idealistic or unrealistic as to be saying that on

Shabbat, nothing is broken, or sad, or somehow not the way we would like it to be. Perfection does not mean that Shabbat is heaven on earth. In fact, while the rabbis do tell us that Shabbat is a taste of the World to Come, it is reckoned to be only one-sixtieth of that other heavenly world.[13] In other words, the other fifty-nine parts are still missing. And yet, the day is still perfect.

The perfection of Shabbat lies in accepting everything that is present in this moment just as it is, calling out to us for no fixing, adjusting, or repair. Our task is to be fully present with the joy of a beloved's company, the pain in the heart from that recent loss, the fine tastes and smells on the table as well as the soup that burned, the radiant flames dancing on the candles along with the wax that dripped onto the tablecloth. This moment contains all of that. And it is perfect just the way it is.

Six days a week, we are busy diagnosing and fixing things, and one day a week our task is to bask in the majestic beauty of the completed creation in all the aspects that happen to be present at that moment. We are looking at a perfect picture when we attune our eyes to see the perfection.

Six days a week we pursue our desires. This is the normal state of affairs for human beings, as we direct our lives and use our energies to acquire money, food, authority, affirmation, pleasure, political goals, and the like. It may be normal, but without a break during which we step back, take rest, and regain perspective, we can develop an inordinate attachment to these things, even a compulsion. Not only that, as we will explore in the next chapter, a life lived entirely from desire offers no satisfaction. We pursue what we feel to be lacking, and that pit has no bottom. A feeling of wholeness and completion in which we lack nothing, living in a perfect moment, can only come to us when we interrupt the endless pursuit fueled by our endless desires and come to rest.

Six days a week we live in a world of deficiency and brokenness. And one day a week, if we choose, we can give ourselves the gift of resting in a world that appears to us as complete and perfect. Not only is labor prohibited on Shabbat, but even conversation about our mundane, workaday problems is meant to be avoided. The guideline is: if you can't do it on Shabbat (like shopping, driving, banking, emailing, etc.), then neither should you talk about it on Shabbat. The effort here is to prevent our minds from being drawn away from the perfection of the day and back into the brokenness and striving of the week.

The most common greeting we offer to people we meet on Shabbat is the phrase "Shabbat Shalom," because Shabbat is meant to be a day of *shalom*—the Hebrew word for "peace." The root of the Hebrew word *shalom* is actually *shalem*—which means "whole," and it refers to anything that is complete, perfect. Shabbat is a time to experience the feeling that all is perfect.

This was a teaching of the Sforno, the Italian Torah commentator from the fifteenth and sixteenth centuries, who explained the verse (Exodus 31:17), "And on the seventh day God rested and was refreshed" by saying, "Now the work was complete [*shalem*], and with wholeness comes rest."

On the seventh day, God took a soulful breath, so to speak, because all was complete; all was perfect. We, too, are invited to step back from our focus on what's deficient or broken in everything, as well as from our desires, to declare our work complete; it is perfect. And then we take a soulful breath, and rest.

As we have learned, God did not just rest on the seventh day but actually created rest on that day. Since that is our model for our own practice of Shabbat, we, too, need to create the conditions for rest on our own seventh days. You can get a taste of the importance of attitude toward rest through this thought exercise.[14]

Imagine that it is a warm, sunny day, and you are sitting in a comfortable chair by the side of the ocean, being fanned by a caressing breeze. You are reclining comfortably, gazing out, lulled by the waves that are gently rolling onto the shore. As far as your eye can see, there is deep blue ocean, bright sky, wheeling birds, and a shining sun. Everything is perfect. You are at rest.

Now imagine that you are in the exact same location with the exact same conditions, but now you are worrying about an upcoming meeting, project, or deadline. Or perhaps you are feeling that what you are doing is a waste of time, that you should be doing something more "productive." Instead of the serene sound of the waves rolling onto the shore, that noisy ocean becomes an irritant, and you wish it would go away.

The notion that everything is perfect on Shabbat is not meant to be a verifiable fact but, as we have seen previously, a chosen and adopted inner attitude. Or, if you will, an "as if." We have the power to make the choice to conduct our day "as if" it were perfect.

Seeing Shabbat as a day of perfection leads directly to the experience of rest.

Returning on Shabbat

We have already related the word "*shabbat*" to the meaning of "to cease." A second possibility connects the word "*shabbat*" to the Hebrew *lashuv*, which means "to return.[15]

Shabbat rolls around every seven days in an unending cycle to which we return, week after week. The cycles of time return us to the seventh day like clockwork, but Shabbat implies another kind of return as well.

During the six days of the week, we put great effort into shaping and steering our own lives. When Shabbat arrives and we put down those burdens and set aside our ambitions, we return to the awareness that, although our input is required, we do not ultimately control anything in the world. Not only are we not in control, but we can open our eyes to see where the locus of control actually does lie.

This idea is neatly summed up in a statement by Rabbi Eliyahu Dessler, the prominent Mussar teacher from the first half of the twentieth century whom we met earlier:[16]

> By "rest" we do not mean the dead state of inaction and laziness. This indeed is the antithesis of true being. We mean rest from the perpetual turmoil of material demands. This still center within the hurricane of life is the essence of the spirit. Here we make contact with God's revealed presence in the world.

When we cease from productive activity on Shabbat, our rest testifies to God's presence in creation. By desisting from using our will to master the physical world, we return to our awareness that all that takes place in our lives is not simply the result of the efforts we make with our own hands.

When I taught a course on rest and transformation, one participant grasped from her own experience how rest can open the way for a return to awareness of the presence of the divine in the world, saying:

> I used to think you didn't buy things on Shabbat because there is a rule that says not to. I now know that it is because one can wrap oneself in the energy of Shabbat and truly rest on all levels. Becoming aware and intending to come closer to the One Above has been a joy.

And there is another dimension of "return" that is also brought on by rest on Shabbat, and that is the return to your own true self. All the doing, going, accumulating, divesting, thinking, planning, worrying, etc., that clutters our existence in the world of the mundane, exiles us far from our essential nature. Through divesting of all that and coming to rest, you can return to a refreshed connection to the deepest truth of who you are.

Rabbi Steinsaltz, whom I quoted above, identifies the return to your true self with connection to one's divine essence, one and the same:

> It is possible to return to something much more intimate and basic—namely, to ourselves. A person's true self, like the essence of every creature in the world, is immeasurably deep and broad, and underlying every essence and transcending it is divinity itself. To return to the divine essence means to be more independent, to deepen one's self-awareness, understanding, and perception of one's essential nature.[17]

With that kind of "return to our true self" in sight, we can better understand why rest is the foremost commandment of the Sabbath day. It's only when we stop leaning forward and hurtling ahead that we can rock back onto our true center of gravity and be truly present with who we are in our deepest essence, as opposed to who or what we strive to become in our lives.

Six days a week we ride a rollercoaster, and the seventh day is the time when we glide into the station and come to rest. That weekly station is where we are able to re-connect—returning to our Ultimate Source and to our personal spiritual core. This return is made possible by bringing ourselves and our lives to a state of rest.

Learning to Rest

When the physician and writer Oliver Sacks was approaching the end of his life, he reflected on what he found himself thinking about as his time drew close:[18]

And now, weak, short of breath, my once-firm muscles melted away by cancer, I find my thoughts, increasingly, not on the supernatural or spiritual, but on what is meant by living a good and worthwhile life—achieving a sense of peace within oneself. I find my thoughts drifting to the Sabbath, the day of rest, the seventh day of the week, and perhaps the seventh day of one's life as well, when one can feel that one's work is done, and one may, in good conscience, rest.

Sacks casts the practice of resting every seventh day as a rehearsal for death. Shabbat can be that, and more as well, because while it is certain that in death all our frantic doing will be put to rest, rest is also essential for living.

Rest is so fundamental to the Shabbat experience that without rest, there is no Shabbat. With practice, a person can get quite good at entering the state of rest, and as that proficiency develops, you acquire the ability to bring yourself to repose at any time of your choosing. And not just *menucha*, but the quality of inner equanimity that I introduced earlier as *menuchat ha'nefesh*—the soul at rest. Shabbat is the training ground for learning and practicing equanimity, an inner quality that proves useful and helpful to us throughout our entire lives.

Practicing rest on Shabbat teaches us how to stay on an even keel even as the waters are raging on both sides. We learn how to guide ourselves into an oasis of peace in the midst of the storm. When that lesson takes root in our hearts, we become people who have learned how to stay calm under fire and who can act according to our free will and higher values, even when strong emotions like fear, anger, worry, envy, and the like are coursing through us.

Rabbi Shlomo Wolbe, the great Mussar teacher of the last generation who died in 2005, goes so far as to say that developing equanimity is actually the goal toward which all spiritual practice is directed.[19]

This is said clearly in the words of the psychologist Peter Vajda,[20] who certainly did not have Shabbat practice in mind when he wrote:

> Equanimity allows us to stand in the midst of conflict or crisis in a way where we are balanced, grounded and centered. It allows us to remain upright in the face of the strong winds of conflict and crisis, such as: blame, failure, pain, or disrepute—the winds that set us up for suffering when they begin to blow. Equanimity protects us from being blown over and helps us stay on an even keel.

It may be for this reason that the nineteenth-century Mussar leader, Rabbi Simcha Zissel Ziv, known as the Alter of Kelm, is quoted as having said, "There is no pleasure greater than a clear mind, because through that one comes to equanimity, and that pleasure is unparalleled."[21]

Shabbat is your opportunity to create an oasis of rest and quiet in your inner life. Instruction on how to take hold of that opportunity by making it your practice is given to us in a phrase that Rabbi Menachem Leffin coined in his nineteenth-century book, *Cheshbon HaNefesh*:[22] "Rise above events that are inconsequential—both bad and good—for they are not worth disturbing your equanimity."

From the perspective of Shabbat, that includes pretty much everything we ordinarily get worked up about, whether because we are excited by something desirable that happens or depressed by something we find not to our liking. It can be eye-opening to see how that vital issue that presses so insistently on Friday afternoon is still there waiting patiently on Saturday evening, only by then it doesn't seem nearly so urgent—that is, if it hasn't already worked itself out!

This was the experience of the novelist and playwright Herman Wouk, who wrote about his own Shabbat observance.[23] When a play was in rehearsal,

Friday afternoon . . . inevitably seems to come when the project is tottering on the edge of ruin. I have sometimes felt guilty of treason, holding to the Shabbat in such a desperate situation. But then, experience has taught me that a theater enterprise almost always is in such a case. Sometimes it does totter to ruin, and sometimes it totters to great prosperity, but tottering is its normal gait, and cries of anguish are its normal tone of voice.

So I have reluctantly taken leave of my colleagues on Friday afternoon, and rejoined them on Saturday night. The play has never collapsed in the meantime. When I return I find it tottering as before, and the anguished cries as normally despairing as ever. My plays have encountered in the end both success and failure, but I cannot honestly ascribe either result to my observing the Shabbat.

Wouk had to develop great mental strength to be able to walk away from his own production at such an apparently crucial moment. Mussar provides us with tools to develop those sorts of qualities, and one such technique with a deep pedigree in the Mussar world is the practice of what are called *kabbalot*, which means "resolutions." The singular—*kabbalah*—is the same word that names the Jewish mystical tradition, though the way the term is used in regard to Mussar practice has nothing to do with that other *Kabbalah*.

Your mind is a powerful tool that you can put to use by resolving to act in one way and not another. You won't always succeed, but having a *kabbalah* in mind provides you with a directive, and as you act on it time and again, eventually it will have the desired effect.

To bring equanimity into your Shabbat experience, you can resolve—that is, take on the *kabbalah*—that whatever happens to you and around you on Shabbat, you will ride the experience as if you were a boat rising and falling on the waves but remaining upright and unperturbed. Resolve to float on an even keel, even as circumstances are churning all around you.

Or, to invoke another image, resolve to be like a surfer staying upright on the crest of the wave, even as it surges and retreats in front of you.

Make that resolution, and work at doing as you resolved. Then see if you can tuck some of the experience you have on Shabbat into your pocket, so to speak. When a trying situation arises during the maelstrom of the week, reach into that inner pocket to draw out some of the equanimity that you banked on Shabbat. See if it helps you cope with whatever life throws your way.

As for your journal, begin by writing your *kabbalah*—including the goal of "rising above" for Shabbat—into your journal. As you will see, the very act of writing will have the effect of strengthening the resolution you set for yourself.

Then, on Saturday evening, record in your journal whatever instances you experienced that Shabbat that challenged your equanimity, whether positive (enjoyable) or negative (undesirable), and ask yourself:

Did you find that you were able to "rise above" the experience or did it suck you under?

What conclusions do you draw?

3

Enoughness

It's Enough

The personal quality that comes into focus here is the trait the Mussar teachers call in Hebrew *histapkut*,[1] which can be translated as "sufficiency," or even more literally (though maybe a bit awkwardly) as "enoughness." It also conveys a sense of "simplicity" and "contentment."

The term *histapkut* is sometimes extended to be *histapkut b'muat*, which means "being satisfied with less." That does not mean being content with less than you need or deserve because that sort of self-denial is not part of normative Judaism, both for reasons of upholding justice and for spiritual reasons. Rather, the term points to being the kind of people who are satisfied not with less than we need but with less than we want, because for most of us, our desires usually far outstrip our actual needs.

Wanting more than we need shows up in many ways in our lives. Many of us wear that phenomenon around our waistlines, but the clutter in our homes and the volume of trash we discard are also reflections of the same root issue. Equally significant is the suffering that comes into our lives when we give ourselves over to pursuing our desires. As the Talmud says, when we feed our desires, far from gaining contentment, all we get is even more hunger.[2]

Rabbi Elya Lopian,[3] a Mussar teacher of the late twentieth century, used an analogy to explain why seeking to fulfill our desires is a losing proposition as far as contentment is concerned. He says that someone who is constantly seeking to satisfy their desires is like a person who is very thirsty and drinks brine to quench their thirst. The more one drinks of it, the stronger one's thirst becomes.[4]

A very old source points toward what it takes to gain the kind of inner fulfillment we seek. In *Pirkei Avot*,[5] the sage Ben Zoma is quoted as asking, "Who is rich?" In other words, what are the conditions in life that make a person feel like they are living with abundance? His answer is, "The person who rejoices in their portion."[6] The wealthy person is not the one who has the most money or stuff, but the person who experiences and even celebrates the "enoughness" of what they do have in their life.

That's the basis for a story that is told in a thirteenth-century Mussar source, *The Book of Middot,* by Rabbi Yechiel the physician.[7] In the chapter on *histapkut*, the author relates that

> a king once said to a certain sage: "If you only asked it, I would provide for you for your entire life." The sage replied, "Why should I ask? I am richer than you are!" The king asked, "How are you richer than me?" The sage answered, "Because I am more contented with the little I have than you are with all that you have."

Feeling contented can't be a reflection of how much you actually possess because, as another old source insightfully tells us, the game of acquisition is never finished and never leads to satisfaction. The rabbinic commentary on the book of Ecclesiastes says, "One who has one hundred wants two hundred, and one who has two hundred wants four hundred."[8] And that same source is even more pointed: "People never leave this world with even half their desires fulfilled."

The most profound and lasting feelings of wealth and satisfaction are actually spiritual and are available only to people who are able to step away from their earthly desires and toward enjoying their "portion," whatever that might be. We can only savor our portion when we put a halt to our quest for more.

We find an example of *histapkut* in the famous biblical story of the *manna* that sustained the Jewish people in the desert for forty years. This mysterious food that fell from the skies every day was basically tasteless and colorless. It sustained life, but it wasn't sushi or pizza, and it was the only item on the menu. You could not ask for it in one variety or another. You just got what you got.

It was a trial for the people to have to survive on the monotonous *manna*, and some rebelled against it. Their griping was significant enough to warrant being recorded in the Torah:[9]

> The rabble with them began to crave other food, and again the Israelites started wailing and said, "If only we had meat to eat! We remember the fish we ate in Egypt at no cost—also the cucumbers, melons, leeks, onions and garlic. But now our whole being is dried up; there is nothing at all except this *manna* before our eyes!"

Ultimately, however, they accepted the *manna* as a gift from God, recognizing that they were being called upon to put aside their greed and to be satisfied with this food that may have been bland but was nevertheless effective in satisfying their basic human need for nutrition.

This is the lesson of the *manna* drawn by Rambam,[10] arguably the most influential Torah scholar of the Middle Ages, who said:

> A person who does not possess something that is not needed for survival is not missing anything indispensable, as with the *manna*,

of which "one who gathered a great deal had nothing in excess, and a person who gathered little had no lack: they gathered every person according to their eating."[11]

Because "enough" was the correct way to measure the food.

The *manna* is the classic case that gets cited by many Mussar masters. There are, as well, many more modern examples because, in our generation, material possessions, consumption, and the pursuit of luxuries have come to rule the world, and most of us with it, with enormous negative consequences, for ourselves as well as for society.

Once we felt quite certain that the kids would not be returning to the nest, my wife and I downsized from our family home. The thirty years we had lived in that fairly large house gave us plenty of time and space for possessions to accumulate, and that they did. So, before we moved, we did a ruthless purge of our possessions, getting rid of everything we did not need or to which we did not have a strong sentimental attachment.

When we moved into our new and smaller home and began to unpack, however, we found all kinds of things in the boxes that we could not fathom why we had kept. We didn't need them, we did not even like them, we had no attachment to them. And yet, they had survived the purge and there they were in the boxes. And so, we did a second round of purging.

How did our lives get so cluttered with stuff we did not need or even want? I think it is very unlikely that someone broke into our house in the middle of the night and stored all their things in our basement. It seems inescapable that we had a role in building up that trove of uselessness. And we did that by devoting so much time, energy, and resources to pursuing and acquiring stuff.

In earlier eras, most people struggled to meet their basic needs, while in our generation, the situation is generally the opposite. Poverty is still with us, but it affects only a minority. Most of us are not only able to satisfy our basic needs but also find ourselves spending hours of every day tending to our things and then acquiring even more—because we want them. But do we actually need them?

Is there a room in your home that you don't let visitors see? Are some drawers and closets so stuffed that they barely open? Do you have to sweep away a pile of debris before a passenger can find a place to sit in your car? Or in your dining room?

While the primary function of the household garage is ostensibly to house cars, a recent survey found that for one out of four Americans, the garage is so cluttered and disorganized that there is no space to park a car.[12] A similar study in Los Angeles found that "cars have been banished from 75 percent of garages to make way for rejected furniture and cascading bins and boxes of mostly forgotten household goods."[13]

The deluge of accumulation under which we are drowning is so much more than an inconvenience. Researchers have documented that instead of all that stuff being a source of enjoyment, it actually makes us stressed and anxious.[14]

Dealing with the problem of having too much stuff has led to the birth of a "tidying up" movement. Books and programs to help people sort through and pare down their possessions have become very popular, as many people have come to recognize that the sheer volume of the things they live with is a problem in need of a solution.

Tidying up is certainly worth doing, but how long does it take before that newly opened space on the shelf gets crammed with more stuff that somehow wandered in, looking for a home? Tidying up may deal temporarily with the mess, but it does not address the root cause of the problem, which is the free rein we give to our desires that push us to be so acquisitive in the first place.

We fall prey to thinking, "If I only had that latest smartphone, that car, that house, that bag, that (fill in the blank for yourself) . . . *then*

I'll be content." Yet there is always something new and better showing up on the horizon. The flames of desire are fanned by advertising that is designed to make us feel somehow deficient because we don't yet own that newest or most useful thing some famous person endorses. Those messages send us off again, chasing after the next acquisition.

The same situation plays out not only with things but also with activities. Once I finish writing this note, balancing this account, answering these emails, reading this report . . . *then* I'll be content.

The problem is that feelings of satisfaction that come from acquiring or completing something are inevitably fleeting. And when they pass, as they surely will, that inner urge to do, build, acquire, or create revs up its motor within us once again, and we plunge back into the endless, tumultuous cycle of creating and acquiring.

When our lives are consumed by attempts to satisfy a never-ending flow of desires, we have no access to the deeper and lasting contentment that comes not from acquiring things or accomplishing tasks but from slowing down enough to savor the present moment in its rich fullness. Only when we stop running after things can our minds come to rest in a spacious stillness that invites us to bask in the holy radiance that hovers barely beyond the boundaries of consciousness, just waiting to be let in.

This uniquely modern problem has led to books being published in the last few years with titles like:

- *Stuffocation* (James Walton, Spiegel & Grau, New York, 2015)

- *Empire of Things* (Frank Trentmann, Harper, New York, 2016)

- *Possessed* (Bruce Hood, Oxford University Press, Oxford, 2019)

And before that, there was the prescient *Affluenza: The All-Consuming Epidemic* (2001, revised in 2014 by DeGraaf, Wann, and Naylor, Berrett-Koehler Publ., Oakland), which defines the supposed condition of "affluenza" as "a painful, contagious, socially transmitted condition of overload, debt, anxiety and waste resulting from the dogged pursuit of more."

All that "more" ends up in garbage dumps that are bursting with discarded clothing, carpets, tires, footwear, sheets, and towels. According to the American Environmental Protection Agency,[15] in 1960, Americans sent 88.1 million tons of solid waste to landfills, and by 2018 that amount had more than tripled to 292.4 million tons, which works out to 4.9 pounds per person per day. In 2020, the Council for Textile Recycling reported that the average consumer disposes off seventy pounds of textiles per year.[16]

The oceans are getting clogged with plastic. Even outer space is experiencing the clutter of so many abandoned space vehicles and satellites. The root of all these problems is human consumption and grasping for more. Each one of us can contribute to improving the world by learning to be content with what we have, seeing it as sufficient, and not acquiring more than we need. This has long been recognized as a spiritual virtue. It is essential to observing Shabbat. But in our day and age, it might also be a key to the sustainability of our planet.

Having It All on Shabbat

The practice on Shabbat is to acquire nothing, build nothing, sell nothing, and buy nothing. Working, earning, and acquiring material goods and accomplishments are what you are meant to do six days of the week. And then comes the seventh, when you are invited to step out from under the dominion of your cravings and develop the inner strength to rule over your desires.

That capacity is essential for Shabbat because freeing our minds and our hands from their usual activities makes them available to focus on rest, spirituality, communing with the One Above, a day of holiness and enjoyment, a day of pleasure, a day of perfection, a day that is a taste of the World to Come.[17] None of that could be possible for us if we were to be as engaged with email, shopping, making, doing, and struggling on Shabbat as we tend to be on Tuesday and Thursday.

On the seventh day of creation, once everything that was to be done had been finished, God ceased from creating. The actual biblical verse reads:[18]

By the seventh day God had finished the work God had been doing; so on the seventh day God ceased from all the work God had done.

The word in Hebrew that is translated as "finished" or "completed" is *vayechal*[19] which comes from the common Hebrew word "*kol*,"[20] which means "all." By the end of the sixth day, God had done it "all."

That same word "*kol*" shows up in biblical verses that tell us that all three of the patriarchs of Judaism had a sense of completion in what they had acquired.[21] They saw themselves as being in possession of everything they could possibly need or want. In their eyes, they had it all.

That point is highlighted by contrasting the outlook of Jacob, who made the statement, "I have everything,"[22] to that of his twin brother, Esau, who said something slightly different. His statement was "I have plenty."[23]

"Everything" is absolute and says that not a single thing is missing. The feeling of being completely satisfied has been reached.

"I have plenty," in contrast, is a report that reveals that something is still lacking. In his eyes, all the good he possesses amounts to only a portion of what he wants. It says: I have a lot, but I could use more. He is not satisfied; he is still seeking to acquire more.

Although it is not so clear in the Bible itself, the rabbis who interpreted the text developed the picture of Esau as the embodiment of evil. In one place,[24] the Talmudic sage, Rabbi Yochanan, says that on the very day that his grandfather, Abraham, died, Esav went out and committed five grave sins. The text there refers to him as "that evildoer." And when Esau sells his birthright to Jacob, the Torah describes him as being consumed by hunger to the point that he feared he would die.

Jacob, progenitor of the Jewish people, expresses a sense of satisfaction, while his brother reveals himself to be a rapaciously hungry sinner. It is clear which model we are supposed to follow. God created the template for our own observance of Shabbat by ceasing from work on that primal seventh day, and when we add to that the model of Abraham, Isaac, and Jacob's sense of sufficiency, we are guided to enter our day of rest with the attitude that our personal world has reached a state of absolute completion, and all our creative work is done.

But isn't this just a fiction? Surely when Friday evening descends and the stars appear in the night sky, there will be unfinished projects waiting for us to resume once again. We may close the file we were working on, but the issue is still not completed nor resolved. There may be weeks or months of work yet to do on that craft project or construction or installation. Where is the completion, and where is the sense that there is nothing more to do?

The answer is found by looking more closely at our template for Shabbat, God's creation of the world. On the seventh day, the work of creation was declared finished and done, but was it really so? In fact, the evidence points to creation not actually being completed after six days. Creation is really an ongoing process, even in the present.

That sounds like heresy! God didn't finish creating everything in six days? But it is not such a radical idea. Even in the daily synagogue prayers, we acknowledge the continuing process of creation. In the blessings that are recited before the liturgical declaration of monotheism, the *Shema*, the prayer book says:

God in God's goodness renews daily, continuously, the work of creation.[25]

That acknowledgment is followed by the verse from the Torah that supports this idea:

[Give thanks] to the One Who makes the great luminaries [i.e., the sun and the moon], for God's kindness endures forever.[26]

This verse from Psalm 136 speaks to the notion of ongoing creation because the verb is stated in the present tense, not the past: God is continually recreating the sun and the moon and everything that is under and beyond them, because creation is a dynamic and unceasing process.

For something to continue to exist, it must be undergoing a constant state of creation. This is true from a theological perspective but also scientifically, because if the energy at the center of its molecules were not being constantly replenished, any physical thing would disintegrate and cease to exist.

We can also see the ongoing nature of creation in the transformation of species. We know that some species change over time, but it is also a fact that even in our own era, new species have emerged.

That's the case with the marbled crayfish that was discovered in Madagascar in the late 1990s.[27]

Once its DNA was sequenced and traced, it appears that the first occurrence of this species was in Germany in 1995, when some traders in exotic species brought crayfish from Florida to Germany to sell to collectors. The crayfish were shipped from North America to Europe in the cargo section of the airplane, and it is thought that maybe the very low temperature in the hold brought about a mutation, turning its predecessor into what came to be called the marbled crayfish.

The new species looks a lot like its progenitor, but the genetic mutations that occurred introduced differences, including the fact that the marbled crayfish can reproduce asexually, with females basically cloning themselves. Analysis of marbled crayfish DNA from across Europe and Africa showed that all these crayfish are clones—with identical genomes the world over—and all are females.

The marbled crayfish did not exist before 1995. The work of creation is ongoing.

But how can we square that knowledge with the teaching that after six days, God declared creation complete? The answer is that creation was not complete in an absolute sense, but it was *declared* complete *for that moment*, in order that the seventh day would be one of rest. It was not that God had wrapped up every final detail of every aspect of creation for all time and had finally earned a day of rest; rather, it was that in order to rest, God declared creation finished, for the moment.

And that situation parallels our own. When we welcome in Shabbat on Friday evening, as day gives way to night, we are called upon to set down our creative activities no matter what state of completion they happen to be in. At that moment, it is up to us to make the declaration that those activities are complete *for now*. We have it in our power to declare them complete—as far as we are concerned, and for that moment.

The key point is that we should not need things to be totally finished, wrapped up, and sealed in order to come to rest, because the truth is that as long as we are alive, there will always be more to do. Rather, it is up to us to cultivate the ability to pronounce them done—as far as we are concerned, and for that moment. It's that performative utterance, and not the state of our affairs, that makes rest possible.

Commenting on the verse, "In six days you shall do all your labor,"[28] the commentator Rashi tells us that "when Shabbat arrives, it should appear in your eyes *as if* all your work has been completed, so that you not even think about your affairs."

Rashi is pointing to the fact that what makes rest possible on Shabbat is a shift in attitude. You are being invited to step away from your usual mindset that drives you to make, do, and acquire, and to enter instead into a frame of mind that allows you to see your work *as if* it were all completed.

There is no fiction here. Of course, all your work has not actually been completed down to the last detail. But that reality does not prevent you from choosing to adopt the very real feeling *as if* all your work has been completed, which means taking on an attitude that is mentioned in a rabbinic teaching that Rashi quotes, which says: "in your eyes [it is] *as though* all your work were completed."[29]

We are being told that our rest should not be contingent on bringing all our activities to a state of completion because we know that is never going to happen and, as a result, rest will be impossible. Rather, we are being guided to choose to voluntarily take on the feeling "*as if*," and "to see in your eyes *as though*," our work is complete. This phrasing reveals to us the technique that will make it possible for us to access rest and contentment, on Shabbat but also beyond that one day per week.

What makes it hard to come to rest? Powerful inner drives like ambition, desire, greed, worry, and fear push us to keep on with our activities. When you pronounce all your work and acquiring complete, what you are really saying to yourself is that you refuse to be ruled over by your habits and relentless emotions. You are claiming your power to call your engagement in any activity closed and done for you right then, regardless of the objective state of completion of the task. This practice of drawing a line on acquisitive and creative activity in order to rest on Shabbat requires that you strengthen your ability to rule over your desires, a power that is necessary for Shabbat and a benefit every day of your life.

A third source for the word "shabbat" (in addition to "cease" and "return") is the Hebrew verb which means "to sit."[30] The message is: Take a seat. Settle down. Settle in. Enjoy. When Shabbat arrives, you step away from the desire-driven frenzy of making and acquiring and slip into an attitude that says, "In fact and in truth, what I already have is enough."

What we are talking about here begins with the practice of observing Shabbat but stretches far beyond into many contemporary problems that have their roots in the inability of humanity as a whole to say: enough! No more! Our habits of consumption impact the planet, as producing, transporting, storing, and disposing of an ever-increasing amount of stuff degrade the environment.

Developing *Histapkut*

The fleeting sense of satisfaction that comes from fulfilling a need or desire is insignificant compared to the transcendent and lasting sense of contentment that becomes possible for us when we interrupt the repetitive cycle of desire and acquisition in which we tend to be trapped.

Ideally, you could disrupt the endless grasping just by being careful to distinguish between what you want and what you actually need. That's the message of Rabbi Shlomo ibn Gabirol, the eleventh-century Spanish Jewish poet and philosopher,[31] who advised: "Seek what you need and give up what you do not need. For in giving up what you do not need, you will learn what you really do need." And that will be enough.

Realistically, however, our habits and desires are too ingrained to be uprooted as easily as that. Breaking out of the loop of desiring and acquiring, in which we tend to be caught, requires a more intrusive intervention that has the power to disrupt the cycle itself.

My wife is a palliative care physician and saw that happen in a dramatic way with one of her patients.

The man was a high-powered lawyer. His days in the world were now numbered, and he was at home, propped up in a hospital bed. Scattered around him, however, were his laptop, a fax machine, his smartphone, and whatever else he needed to keep working on the legal files he still had open.

One day near the end, his failing health made it difficult for him to continue working, and something dawned on him as a revelation.

"What needs to be done?" he wondered aloud.

"Nothing," he himself answered.

"Who needs to do it?"

"Nobody."

And then he reached for a description of the experience that followed: "I feel . . . , I feel . . . , I feel . . . ," he said, "such peace."

And maybe for the first time in a very long time, he softened into the feeling of true contentment, connected to the present moment as it was, beyond the drive of desire.

Thankfully, we do not need to wait until we are approaching death to gain his insight, because it can also come to us as a result of practicing a weekly day of rest. Not working and eschewing anything having to do with money—in any form: checks or credit cards or cash—are core Shabbat observances, which call on us to put aside the habitual desires that drive us to achieve and acquire. Shabbat proclaims a freeze on reaching out to grasp the next new thing, and when we take on and abide by that guideline, we find that the capacity to call a timeout from our striving has been strengthened, not just for that one day a week, but throughout our lives.

Rabbi Eliyahu Dessler,[32] the great Mussar teacher of the mid-twentieth century, echoed Rashi's words that we encountered above. When Shabbat rolls around, he says, "of course, on the material level one's work is not done. But on a spiritual level, when Shabbat comes, we should *feel* as if we have nothing more to do; worrying about one's work is now out of the question."[33]

Immediately following that idea, however, he cautions: "This is a spiritual level that is not easy to attain. How can one help thinking about the multitude of things left unfinished which will have to be attended to in the coming week?"

On a practical level, the answer to Rav Dessler's question lies in the fact that any practice we adopt for Shabbat recurs every seventh day, giving us a regular and frequent opportunity to engage with it and get better at it. Once you commit to a day on which you put a hold on all weekday pursuits, be they your work, projects, financial transactions, shopping, or the like, then one day in seven you get a workout that strengthens the inner muscles needed to resist your desires.

At first, that new practice can be difficult and uncomfortable, and the temptation of habit seemingly almost insurmountable. But little by little, week by week, as you make a practice of taking on and committing to that voluntary feeling of completion and satisfaction, over time you can get quite good at calling a halt to activities and defying appetites in order to enter into an attitude of contentment as an act of personal choice.

Whatever your current level of Shabbat observance, there are things you can do to prepare for and support the development of that capacity.

One practice is to reflect—making notes, if it will help—to identify one activity in your routine that you tend to pursue with relentlessness, or at least as a matter of habit, that really does not address any kind of basic need at all but rather a desire.

A good example would be the habit of following a local sports team. I can assure you that the team will get on fine without you for one day. Turning away from your fan-ship for a day will not even change the outcome of a game. And, you'll be able to find out the score a little later.

Or another example would be consuming media. In the old days, if you missed an episode of your favorite television show, you were lost. Now, however, in the world of streaming services, whatever it is that you would have watched will be waiting for you to tune in at another time.

Is it shopping in your case? Or going to the restaurant? Discussing politics? Pursuing your work ambitions? What do you do as a matter of habit that does not address any survival need?

Once you have identified an activity like that, make an undertaking to yourself not to participate in that activity—even in thought!—over Shabbat. As Friday evening approaches, make a conscious pledge to set it down, let it go. Tell yourself that, as far as you are concerned, that activity is totally complete and needs no more attention of any kind. And welcome a feeling of contentment in its place.

Even if you already have a Shabbat practice, if you are honest with yourself, I suspect you'll be able to identify some things you do and topics of conversation you engage in that are, in fact, dispensable because they do not really feed that feeling of perfection and contentment Shabbat can foster.

That's the essential part of the practice. And in time, as this one habit loses its grip on you, as it surely will, you may become aware of other things you do that you can let go of over Shabbat because they are the product of a desire that addresses no real need. Then the feeling of enoughness grows even stronger in you.

Practicing like this requires that you strengthen your intrinsic capacity to say, "enough"—not because the bank account is so full, nor the stomach, not because every ambition has been satisfied and every desire gratified, but because you have both the wisdom and the training to say, "that's enough for now." Standing by that statement strengthens your trait of *histapkut*—inner contentment—and once that quality takes root in you, the grip of desire for unnecessary and sometimes even harmful things will be loosened, and you will have developed the ability to hold them at bay, 365 days of the year.

Write in your journal to track and explore your experiences. As prompts to help you with journaling, consider the following questions:

- During Shabbat, did I encounter any sort of craving for something? Was it for something I needed, or was it, in fact, just a desire?

- Can I possibly detect any feelings of envy for what another person has that I do not?

- In truth, do I really lack anything that is important for my life?

- Did I make any time to experience joy and contentedness for the gifts I already have in my life?

- Did I have any opportunity to acquire something that I let pass by, or denied?

These are just suggestions to get you going. Reflect on your own experience and make notes in your journal. And don't worry about how much you write. Just enough will do.

4

Joy

Happiness and Joy

The words happiness and joy tend to be used interchangeably, but, in fact, they can label two very different inner experiences, and we can learn a significant lesson about our inner lives by highlighting the differences—naming one "happiness" and the other "joy."

In simple terms, happiness is that transient feeling of uplift and ebullience that comes from fulfilling or experiencing something that you really want and like.

Joy is also a feeling of expansive and positive uplift, but it is very different from happiness because it is sparked not by getting something you desire, but by experiences that actually transcend anything you might personally want.

Happiness is an inner experience at the level of our personal self, with its wants and desires, while joy penetrates us more deeply, transcending our personal selves to touch us at the deeper, more spiritual, more eternal level of the soul.

Happiness gratifies the ego; joy transcends it.

Happiness makes you smile; joy makes you cry.

Our culture is preoccupied with happiness. The pursuit of happiness is inscribed in the US Declaration of Independence, and there is a push to have countries replace the index of Gross National Product with a Gross National Happiness Scale, as the small kingdom of Bhutan has already done. Banks, retirement communities, cruise lines, talk shows, and investment firms all sing the same tune, telling us that all the work, the saving, the debt, the sacrifice, and struggle will, at some future point, pay off, because then—then!—you will be able to have everything you want, and that will make you happy.

We believe it. We have been blessed to live in an era of such rapid technological innovation that we've come to believe that with the right technology and sufficient political will and resources, every problem can be solved, every obstacle overcome. And when that happens, then we will be happy.

But the truth is that happiness is, at best, transient. Has it been your experience that having health, enough wealth and the newest technology delivers lasting happiness? We just have to look at the super-rich and adored celebrities to see that attaining worldly goals is no guarantee of a happy life.

That should not surprise us because happiness is a feeling of buoyant well-being that arises *when you get what you want*—and therein lies the defect. Getting what you want makes you happy for the moment, but the vast majority of the time, what you want is beyond your immediate grasp, and you find yourself mired in feelings of deficiency and desire that drive you to pursue the goal.

And even when you do eventually get something you have sought, you will have spent 95 percent of your time in the unhappy state of wanting and only a small remainder enjoying the happiness of success.

Even then, even if you have been fortunate and attained the thing you were pursuing, the glow and pleasure of happiness wear off very soon. The new quickly becomes old, the novel settles into routine, fresh desires announce themselves, and you climb back in the saddle and ride off down the trail of wanting and pursuing something else, and not being happy.

How familiar is the refrain, "if only _____, I'd be happy," and you can fill in the blank yourself. But just ask the people who have won big lottery prizes or even Academy Awards if the happiness lasted. They will tell you that it does not, because by its nature, happiness is conditional, dependent, and transitory.

Joy is so different because it has absolutely nothing to do with any sort of achievement or attainment. We experience joy when something penetrates to a level of our being that is so much deeper and more profound than the part of us that wants that car, or that job, or that invitation, or that recognition, or that bauble, or whatever else we pursue in our lives and on which we pin our hopes for happiness.

I can give two examples from my experience, and I am sure you will have some of your own because we all have had moments in our lives when we were electrified by the charged experiences of joy.

It's a cliché, but nevertheless true, that being with children can be a source of joy for many people. When I look into the eyes of one of my grandchildren, or she or he rests their head on my shoulder, or they get one of my jokes and laugh, I want nothing more from this universe.

These are my grandchildren, after all. I am not responsible for all the practical details of their lives because it falls to their parents to oversee homework, tooth brushing, and everything else that goes into raising children. I may get happiness from their triumphant piano recital, but the joy I get from them comes from the encounter between my soul and their very beings, not from what they do but from the miraculous fact that they are.

There is a much-used Yiddish word that describes the happiness a parent or grandparent feels in their child's accomplishments, and that word is *nachas*. But joy is something different entirely because it has nothing to do with the brilliance of the child's accomplishments and everything to do with heart connection and unconditional love, even when they fail.

It is for that reason, I think, that so many parents of children with Down Syndrome describe their experience with their child as a source of joy. They don't minimize the challenges and even sorrow that come from having a differently abled child, but they so consistently use that word—joy—that it can't be ignored, even though their kids cannot aspire to the kinds of worldly achievements that other children might. Their reports point to the fact that the source of joy is different from the sources of happiness.

And a second example of experiences of joy you are likely to have had in your own life relates to encounters in nature.

Have you ever found yourself in a moment of stillness in a beautiful place when your heart spontaneously fills with light and joy? That feeling is well known to me from times spent walking among the giant trees of the temperate rainforest in the Pacific Northwest, where I live.

Or it might burst forth in you when you encounter a truly magnificent creature in the wild—a whale, an elephant, an eagle. Or a fabulous technicolor sky. Or an astonishing seashell protruding from the sand. I am sure you have your own story of an encounter with nature that overtook you, and the result was that your heart was suffused with boundless joy.

That soaring feeling that erupts in these situations is nothing we earn. It has nothing to do with the happiness and satisfaction that come from anything we achieve through our own efforts. Joy in encountering the natural world comes from beyond our limited selves, and it touches a part of ourselves that also exists beyond the boundaries of self and identity.

Joyful Sabbath

The joy that we feel when we connect to a child or have an encounter in nature just sweeps over and through us. The same is meant to be true for joy on Shabbat, though on Shabbat we can take steps to create the circumstances that invite joy to flow into us. Through this lens, we can see that some of the prescriptions and activities that are a matter of deliberate practice on Shabbat are conditioners that open the way for joy to come our way.

Consider, for example, the effect we create by shutting off everything that beeps at us—phone, computer, social networks, news. The first words in the chapter on "joy" in the sixteenth-century Mussar classic, *Orchot Tzaddikim* [*Ways of the Righteous*], are:

> The trait of joy comes to a person through the enjoyment of great tranquility in their heart.

The tranquility that *Orchot Tzaddikim* speaks of remains a stark impossibility for me as long as I am caught up in the chatter of the world that swirls around me, and the chirping of the ego and its desires that roil within me almost continuously. I find myself anything but tranquil when my thoughts and feelings are agitated by what comes in through my eyes and ears, as well as the usual commotion that characterizes my striving, dissatisfied inner life. And when tranquility is out of reach, so is joy.

But it seems obvious that Shabbat should be a day of joy. Just breaking free of the relentless cycles of desire, work, and accumulation that dominate our lives and deplete our souls would be enough reason to rejoice. And, indeed, the synagogue liturgy points in that direction. There is a prayer that is part of the regular order of prayers on Shabbat afternoons that is called *Yismechu*, which means, "They will rejoice." The prayer begins:

> Those who observe Shabbat and call it a delight shall rejoice in Your realm.

This prayer reminds us that observing Shabbat is meant to be a source of joy and delight. The words of the prayer have been set to many upbeat and energetic melodies meant to convey the joy and delight to which it refers.

But despite all that, we can puzzle over the fact that among the seemingly endless commandments that govern every aspect of Shabbat, there does not appear to be a commandment to be joyful. Joy is indeed something that is considered a commandment for the holidays,[1] but not for Shabbat.

Our Sages do find a biblical source that they associate with joy on Shabbat. A verse in the book of Numbers (10:10) refers to blowing trumpets on "the day of your joy." A rabbinic teaching[2] tells us that this verse is referring to Shabbat.

And we do find that the earliest compilation of Jewish law, dating back to the eighth century,[3] enumerated a commandment to engage in "the joy and pleasure of Shabbat."

But these sources are not a strong foundation for establishing Shabbat as a day of joy. The fact that this is the best the rabbis could come up with reveals how hard they were working to find a textual source because they really wanted Shabbat to be characterized as a day of joy.

It seems to me that they needn't have gone to such lengths to find a commandment to be joyful on Shabbat because we don't need one.

Relieving ourselves of all the engagements and activities, the worries and the responsibilities of our daily life should be enough to set any of us dancing with joy. In fact, that is exactly what can happen. Once you escape the grip of the very sorts of things that the traditional observance of Shabbat takes out of the picture of our lives—work, money, shopping, building, acquiring, fixing, and the like—you will find that you have thrown overboard the ballast that keeps you weighted down, and your heart is set free to experience tranquility and, through that, to soar in joy. Just stepping back from the email, the business, the making and the building, and the worldly goings-on opens up a pathway to joy.

That's a perspective from the negative side, in the sense that joy can be an outcome of what we do *not* do on Shabbat. There is a positive side as well because, while joy is not prescribed for us on Shabbat, delight and pleasure, denoted by the Hebrew word *oneg*, certainly are.[4] By doing things that give us delight, we can trigger the groundswell of joy that can surge through our lives and lift our hearts on Shabbat.

Taking pleasure can be a positive and intentional act, and we have the ability to create the conditions we then enjoy. We can provision the house with fine food and drink and invite people we like to join us at the beautifully arrayed table to delight in the baking, cooking, and serving we do. We can sing and bless. And, freed from phones and media, we can take pleasure in leisurely conversation and connection.

Relieved of the drudgery and pressures of everyday life, and surrounded by things that give us pleasure, we have placed ourselves squarely in a place that invites joy to come flowing our way.

That notion is reinforced by another factor through which Shabbat practice intersects with joy, and that is the notion of completeness. We already encountered the idea of wholeness or completeness on Shabbat in Chapter 2. We can see that completeness has a role in the context of joy as well. I touched on that in something I wrote elsewhere:[5]

Moments come when the heart dances in the light. So much more than the experience of fun or even happiness, joy erupts when the inner sphere scintillates in its completeness. An experience touches us to the depths of our souls, and in that moment we are graced with a vision—if only fleetingly—of the flawless wholeness and perfection of it all. Then the heart fills and flows over, even amid the brokenness of this world.

Shabbat is just such a time. Completion was the condition of the world when God finished all the acts of creation that took place in six days, topped off by the creation of rest on the seventh. And we similarly declare our world complete when we enter Shabbat.

Rabbi Avi Fertig says it plainly:[6]

On Shabbos, all is perfect and complete.

Is it really perfect? As we concluded in Chapter 2, no, of course it isn't, but we have the ability to *declare* it perfect and complete, and that declaration, taken to heart, makes it so.

When we enter Shabbat, we declare to ourselves that we are living in a condition of perfection and completeness, without striving. We weave into our observance sources of pleasure and delight. All of that opens the way to feeling tranquil, which, in turn, is the launching pad for joy.

The Soul of Joy

Mussar is a spiritual discipline, and the Mussar teachers and teachings understand our inner life on spiritual terms, as a matter of soul. Since the soul is insubstantial, there is room for different opinions as to the nature of the soul and the number of dimensions it contains, but there

are two basic aspects of the spiritual inner life that I have learned to
see as fundamental. One of these is the inner spiritual dimension
called in Hebrew *nefesh,* and the other is named *neshama.*[7] In English
translations of Hebrew texts, it is standard practice to translate both
words as "soul," which doesn't help us very much, as there is a world
of difference and much meaning in their distinction.

Nefesh refers to the aspects of personal inner life that are
characteristic of each unique human being. Everything that falls within
the boundaries of the ego, including character traits and emotions,
identity, and self-awareness, are all aspects of the *nefesh*-soul.

Because *nefesh* encompasses the you who you think yourself to be,
it is employed to refer to the whole person in their worldly existence.
For example, when Jewish law emphasizes the importance of what is
called in Hebrew *pikuach nefesh*—saving a life—this refers to saving
the entire life of a person from any sort of danger to their existence,
not saving a soul in the spiritual sense.

This understanding is reinforced by the fact that not just humans,
but all animals, are said to have a *nefesh*-soul. In the book of Genesis,
both animals and human beings are referred to as *"nefesh chayah,"* a
living soul. In Genesis 9:4, after we are given permission to eat meat,
we are cautioned not to consume an animal's blood because the blood
is identified with the *nefesh.*

We humans share with all animals the inner aspect called *nefesh,*
but humans are unique in having a *neshama. Neshama* refers to the
spiritual essence of a person, beyond any tangible properties or even
self-awareness. Jewish tradition tells us that the *neshama* is implanted
in a person directly from the divine Throne of Glory.[8] It is created
by being "hewn out" from under that throne, and it continuously
throbs with a pure divine light no matter what the condition of its
companion, the *nefesh*-soul.

That brief overview of these two dimensions of the inner life gives us a foundation for understanding the source of the difference between happiness and joy.

Happiness relates to our desires, tastes, goals, and ambitions, all of which are aspects of the self, and you experience happiness when you get what your personal self wants or needs. Thus, happiness falls squarely into the territory of the *nefesh*.

In contrast, joy lives in the province of the *neshama*. I feel joy when some experience or insight transcends the limited structures of the *nefesh* and hits home, right into the core of my eternal spiritual being. I am touched in a place that is beyond want or need and is, in fact, beyond self. Telling us that the *neshama* derives from God's Throne of Glory conveys the message that the *neshama* is, in its essence, profoundly spiritual and transcendent. In the same way, joy transcends any of the features of the selfhood of a human being.

When we apply that distinction to Shabbat, we can identify the weekdays as the appropriate time to pursue *nefesh*-level happiness because it is on the six days of the week that we busy ourselves running after all the things we need and want. When we achieve our goals or attain our attainments, we are happy. And when we don't, we are sad.

Shabbat is different. On Shabbat, we depart from the mundane and make our escape from the ordinary. As we leave off our usual productive lives to bask in the radiant and perfected present of Shabbat, we make ourselves available to experiences like joy that transcend our usual ways of encountering the other six days of the week.

As deep as the *neshama* may be, what goes on at that level still makes itself visible. The Bible tells us, "So God blessed the seventh day and made it holy,"[9] and the rabbis ask,[10] "How did God bless and make Shabbat holy?" Their answer is that "God sanctified it with the light of people's faces. The light of a person's face throughout the week is not comparable to [its appearance] on Shabbat."

This is exactly what Rabbi Shlomo Wolbe[11] reported about his teacher, Rabbi Yerucham Levovitz, whose face changed so much on Shabbat from how he appeared on a weekday that a new student in the yeshiva deduced that the person whose face glowed so brightly on Shabbat must be a different and greater person from the one who taught them on weekdays. After some time, that student realized that it wasn't another person, but that the atmosphere of Shabbat so penetrated Rabbi Levovitz that his face was illuminated with the light of the holy soul.

As different as the *nefesh* and the *neshama* may be, there is one place where they meet. It is a traditional Shabbat practice to eat and drink at three fine meals between Friday and Saturday evenings. Eating and drinking are surely physical pleasures and so relate to the *nefesh*-soul, which is associated with the physical through its link to the blood. But these pleasures also connect to joy, which is spiritual, and associated with the *neshama*.

We are told that Shabbat is a day of delight, and the rabbis of the Talmud[12] ask: "With what does one delight in the day of Shabbat?"

The Sage Rav Yehuda answered: "With a dish of beets, a large fish, and heads of garlic."

No doubt Rav Yehuda saw that as a very tasty menu, but it pales in comparison to the rapturous description of the traditional Shabbat bean and potato stew known as *cholent* that we find in Heinrich Heine's nineteenth-century ode to the Sabbath:[13]

Cholent, ray of light immortal!
Cholent, daughter of Elysium!"
So had Schiller's song resounded,
Had he ever tasted *cholent*,
For this *cholent* is the very
Food of heaven, which, on Sinai,

God Himself instructed Moses
In the secret of preparing
Yes, this *cholent*'s pure ambrosia
Of the true and only God:
Paradisal bread of rapture;

Has food ever merited more exalted praise? We are called upon to delight on Shabbat, and that means eating and enjoying fine food with pleasure. At the simplest level, having a full belly induces a feeling of satisfaction that brings on the tranquility that invites joy. But there is still more to the role pleasure can play in the spiritual elevation—and joy—that is the essence of Shabbat.

Here we turn for guidance to Rabbi Nosson Tzvi Finkel (1849–1927), the great and influential Mussar teacher also known as the Alter of Slabodka. The Alter saw that pleasure exists on the material and bodily plane and, simultaneously, as a force for spiritual uplift. He makes it perfectly clear that, unlike many of his predecessors and contemporaries, he was not talking about ethereal pleasures we might taste in heaven or a world beyond this one:

> This pleasure does not refer only to the Next World, but also to This World. Every person is surrounded by limitless potential for pleasure and enjoyment. The world and all its details are a source of pleasure. A person's experiences in physical and spiritual areas give one the potential for joy without end.[14]

We have to take special note of the connection he is making between pleasure and joy. Those thoughts reflect the Alter's general view on pleasure, and elsewhere[15] he applies it specifically to Shabbat:

> In what is the holiness of the Sabbath expressed? In pleasure, for we find that we are commanded to guard the Sabbath and

to sanctify it, as in the words of the verse: "Remember the Sabbath day to keep it holy" (Exodus 20:8). And in what way are we obligated to sanctify Shabbat? Through absorbing ourselves in pleasures. Furthermore, we are to call Shabbat by the name of pleasure, as in the words of the prophet, "And call Shabbat pleasure." (Isaiah 58:13)

The Alter is validating the delight that comes from physical pleasures, and that seems risky because it opens up the possibility that a person will give free rein to their appetites and thereby get enmeshed in the physical and material, at the expense of the spiritual. The Alter recognizes that danger and addresses it. He acknowledges that there is a way to enjoy pleasure that is completely physical, but doing that won't yield joy. It is when we frame our pleasure as a spiritual experience, integrated into the perspective that sees us as souls inhabiting a divine-infused world, that pleasure has the potential to be spiritual. In his words:

It is in a person's power to raise even physical matters up to a level of holiness.

He is teaching us that it is possible to engage with the material in a spiritual way. When we encounter the physical with the intention to raise it up to the holy, it is in our power to accomplish that. The Alter is far from the only Jewish teacher to give us this assignment. Many Jewish sources deliver the same message: on the Jewish path, we do not pursue spirituality by being ascetic and turning away from the physical; rather, we turn *toward* the material and the physical, and interact with the tangible world with the consciousness and intention to sanctify it.

This teaching helps us appreciate what is going on in many of the traditions of the Shabbat table. Basic life-sustaining bread is elevated to become *challah*, the universally loved sweet egg-bread of Shabbat. The custom of dusting the *challah* with salt replicates what was done to animal sacrifices when the Temple stood, and raises our bread up to the level of a sacrificial offering. Drink is lifted up into wine. Nutrition ascends into fine dining. A simple fruit is transformed into a tasty dessert. The lowly bean metamorphosizes into a *cholent*. The table rises to become an altar.[16]

If it is our lower selves whom we pull up to the table, all of this can be nothing more than sensory pleasure. But when we come to this pleasure from the level of our holy *neshama*, the delights we conjure on Shabbat can be transcendent. And joy erupts.

Anyone who has looked into the Talmud and Jewish legal codes knows that the rabbis were no prudes when it came to another form of pleasure, which is sexual intimacy. Rambam, the twelfth-century sage, comes right out and says that "Sexual relations are considered a dimension of Shabbat pleasure."[17] He goes on to say that Torah scholars, who are expected to "fulfill their marital obligations" only once a week, were expected to do so on Shabbat.

Some say sex on Shabbat has double value because it fulfills the duty of enjoying the Sabbath as well as the commandment to be fruitful and multiply. The Talmud goes so far in encouraging sex on Shabbat as to prescribe an aphrodisiac. In tractate *Bava Kamma* (82a), we read:

> One should eat garlic Shabbat eve because garlic enhances sexual potency, and Friday night is an appropriate time for conjugal relations. As it is written concerning the righteous: "And he shall be like a tree planted by streams of water, who brings forth his fruit in his season" (Psalms 1:3); and Rabbi Yehuda says . . . : "This is referring to one who engages in sexual intercourse every Shabbat eve."

This physical pleasure is also presented to us as something we can lift up to be spiritual. When we delight in physical pleasure as an act of engagement with the holy, then the most physical, ordinary, and mundane things can be lifted up into the spiritual realm, ascending into holiness and carrying us toward what we call God on the wings of joy.

Shabbat Joy All Week Long

When we enjoy the many pleasures we are encouraged to savor on Shabbat by consciously "lifting them up" to be connected to the holy and to heaven, we give ourselves training in how we can do that same thing all week long. One of the Alter of Slabodka's successors (and son-in-law), Rabbi Yitzchok Isaac Sher, makes this point explicitly:[18]

> From the teachings of our master [the Alter of Slabodka] we learn that this is the way of perfection all year long [and not just on Shabbat]. . . . It is one's obligation to enjoy all the physical pleasures and to recognize, through this—to increase and become complete in this recognition—that one is delighting in God.

In his view, the physical and the spiritual are not separate. The feeling of pleasure is, in its essence, a spiritual experience, so when you smack your lips or feast your eyes, the feelings of pleasure you get are to be recognized as nothing less than delighting in God.

Now we can see clearly how effective Shabbat can be as our training ground for opening to joy. This one day a week, we are guided to free ourselves from the mundane and to engage with physical and material things in such a way that we lift them up to the spiritual realm. The good taste of the soup or the *challah* has the potential to be more than just a sensory pleasure when we receive it with the consciousness that what we call delight is a spiritual reality, and this connects us to the source of all spirits.

As we say in the *Yismechu* prayer:

Those who keep Shabbat and call it a delight will rejoice in Your realm.

From this perspective, when we delight in our experiences, that *is* rejoicing in the divine realm. Shabbat can teach us how to do that, and then, as Rabbi Sher says, "this is the way of perfection all year long."

Getting Good at Being Joyful

Joy can be a spontaneous experience that lands on us unexpectedly, like a colorful bird fluttering down to alight on a branch. But there are also things we can do to prepare ourselves for joy and invite that experience to inhabit us, by seeking tranquility and cultivating our capacity to lift our engagement with what we desire to a higher spiritual level.

We have to be very careful here, of course, to delimit the field of desire to the realm of the permitted. There are many human desires that promise joy and deliver only suffering. Refer to the newspapers for a full range of examples.

The first step in a practice to cultivate joy is to be undertaken before Shabbat: Identify a simple and uncomplicated area of life in which you feel a desire that it is possible to fulfill on Shabbat without transgressing any of the behavioral prohibitions we have already encountered, like spending money or turning on your computer or phone. The sort of desire I am thinking of could be anything from eating to inner tranquility, from visiting with a friend to something else you define.

Then on Shabbat, set yourself to doing that enjoyable thing you have identified, only bring into play the recognition that you are seeking not just sensory gratification but an encounter with the holy. Make an intentional effort in your mind and heart to "lift up" your pleasant experience into the realm of the spiritual so that the pleasure itself serves as a doorway to a higher realm.

See how that goes for you on Shabbat, and also on the days that follow.

For your journaling in this period, consider questions like:

- What makes you happy? What desires get fulfilled to bring on this feeling? Does it last? If not, why not?

- What gives you pleasure? Does your experience tend to be at the physical level, or could you connect it to the spiritual within you?

- Pay attention to moments of joy that have come your way. Can you identify any factors that contributed to fostering those experiences?

- Where did you witness joy in others?

Jot down in your journal anything that relates to the topics we have focused on in this chapter, and you will find new insights coming your way. And, hopefully, more joy as well.

5

Peace and Harmony

Shalom

It is likely that the word *shalom* will be familiar to you—it is perhaps the most widely recognized Hebrew word there is. In its various forms, this word that means "peace" appears no fewer than 237 times in the Torah itself, which is an indication of how important peace is in Jewish thought.

There are so many Jewish sources that praise *shalom* and tell us how important and valuable it is. One that underscores this importance is a rabbinic teaching[1] that quotes the great Rabbi Yehuda haNasi, known as Rebbi:

> Great is *shalom*, for even if the Jews were to practice idolatry, and *shalom* prevailed among them at the same time, God would say, "I cannot punish them because peace prevails among them."

That's truly shocking because idol worship is one of only three cardinal sins in Judaism—the others being murder and forbidden sexual relations—and Jewish law says that a person should readily submit to being killed rather than commit any of these sins. How astounding that Rebbi puts *shalom* on such a high level that it actually nullifies the cardinal sin of idolatry!

To grasp what it might be about *shalom* that raises it to such an exalted level, we first have to understand the basic meaning of the word itself. We usually translate the word *shalom* as "peace," but we must be careful not to equate the peace we are talking about with a mere absence of conflict. I've mentioned previously that the word *shalom* is one of a group of words that are derived from the Hebrew root *shalem*, which means "whole." This signifies that the notion of *shalom* has a much broader and more general foundation than just an absence of open conflict.

To illustrate, the standard way of greeting someone in modern Hebrew is to ask, *Ma sh'lomcha?* (for a male) or *Ma sh'lomeach?* (for a female).[2] The literal question being posed is, "How is your *shalom*?" but it is to be understood as, "How are you?"

Because its root meaning is "wholeness," peace can be understood to be a contingent condition that reflects what is happening in any and all of the dimensions of your life, and so it would be valid to respond to the question by reporting on your sense of completeness in regard to health, welfare, feeling of safety, soundness, tranquility, prosperity, fullness, rest, the presence or absence of agitation or discord in your life, and pretty much anything else that would contribute to or detract from your sense of being at peace.

Of the many nuances and dimensions that are all present in the word *shalom*, I want to highlight one that I prefer because it seems to me to encompass all the others—including "peace"—and that is the notion of "harmony."

I draw this notion from the fifteenth-century Spanish Jewish commentator, Rabbi Yitzchak Arama, who noted that the priestly blessing given in the Torah and frequently repeated in the liturgy, as well as in the blessing of children that is part of welcoming Shabbat, ends with the word *shalom*. He explains that *shalom* does not mean merely the absence of war or strife but rather the harmonious working of a complex system, integrated diversity, a state in which everything is in its proper place, and all is at one with the physical and ethical laws governing the universe.

In his commentary on Pirkei Avot (2:12), Don Isaac Abarbanel, another Torah commentator who also lived in the fifteenth century, only in his case in Portugal, underscores the same understanding when he writes in reference to the tradition that one of God's names is "Shalom"[3]:

> God is called Shalom, because it is God who binds the world together and orders all things according to their particular character and posture. For when things are in their proper order, *shalom* will reign.

To translate *shalom* as "peace" misses the important message conveyed by the sense of wholeness that lies at the root of the word. But "wholeness" is also missing something for me, because we know that it is entirely possible to have all the pieces of something, every element in hand, but it is still not perfect because things have not been set in the right order. You can have all the pieces of a puzzle in the box, which means that the puzzle is "whole," but it is just a jumble; no picture to be seen.

That's why I like the word "harmony." All the pieces are present, and they are organized and ordered into something that is not only whole but also beautiful.

With that notion of *shalom* in mind, I'd like to focus on what we can learn from the practice of Shabbat that helps create the harmony that generates peace, both within ourselves and between us and other people.

Shabbat Shalom

The association of *shalom* with Shabbat is strong. After all, what is the singular way in which people greet each other on Shabbat? Nothing other than "Shabbat Shalom!", a wish for a peaceful Sabbath day.

Based on our exploration of the meaning of the word *shalom*, what we are talking about is not the condition that prevails when two parties stop battling; it is when they come together to make a whole. And therein lies the challenge of practicing *shalom* on Shabbat—we are charged to make and keep things whole in our outer world and in our inner world, since the two are so intimately connected.

And therein also lies one of the rewards of Shabbat, which is tasting what it is like to live in a condition of harmonious wholeness, so different from our ordinarily fragmented lives.

Imagine yourself standing by the Friday night table. The match is burning, ready to kindle the candles that are traditionally lit to welcome in Shabbat. We recall the words that are uttered in the traditional prayers of that evening: *U'fros aleiynu sukkat shelomecha.*

Spread over us Your canopy of peace. Blessed are You, Lord, who spreads the canopy of peace on us and on all of the nation of Israel and on Jerusalem.

The radiant glow of the candles creates the canopy of *shalom* under which we stand. And thus begins our *Shabbat shalom*. Savor the feeling. *Shalom* is something appreciated at least as much by being felt as it is by being known and understood.

It is traditional for parents to bless their children on Friday evening. A parent places their hands on the head of the child and recites a blessing that is followed by the words uttered by the Kohanim, the priests,[4] which ends, "May the radiance of God's Presence shine upon you and bless you with *shalom*."

Then we go to the table, and in many households, the next tradition also focuses on peace as we welcome the angels of Shabbat with the song "Shalom Aleichem."

"Shalom Aleichem" is a traditional song that signals the arrival of Shabbat. The title means "Peace be upon you," and it is with these words that we welcome the angels who accompany a person home on the eve of the Sabbath. We welcome them and ask them to bless us.

In these and other ways, the religious observance of Shabbat focuses on *shalom*. In our home, when our grandchildren are with us for Shabbat, that also includes a rousing chorus of the song "Shabbat Shalom," often accompanied by a few smooth dance moves.

And at the other end of the Shabbat dinner, when we reach the very end of the extended grace recited after eating, the final line is drawn from Psalm 29 and reads: "May God bless God's people with *shalom*."

These could be just ritual invocations of *shalom*, but there are good reasons to think that what is involved here is meant to be more than lip service. The key connection between Shabbat and *shalom* lies in the wholeness that is an essential element of peace and that is also fundamental to Shabbat because, as we have already learned, the reason we do not engage in any sort of productive labor on the seventh day is that nothing needs to be created, added, planned, planted, harvested, or fixed in this world that is perfect just as it is. Indeed, the word *shalem* that I have been relating to the concept of "whole" is often translated as "perfect."

The seventh day is a taste of a world in which wholeness and harmony prevail, and to employ all the linguistic sources that are thought to give rise to the word "shabbat," in ceasing our effort—*l'shbot*—and settling into a deeper dimension of ourselves—*lashevet*—we return—*lashuv*—to the taste and delight of the delicious experience of peace on Shabbat.

One of the primary characteristics of Shabbat we are enjoined to foster is called *shalom bayit*, which means "harmony in the house." When we pray for *shalom* or include it in our rituals, it can't be just for the sake of the world "out there"; *shalom* needs to begin at home.

We get a clear message about the importance of harmony in the home in the Talmud[5] when the rabbis consider the problem faced by a person who has only enough oil to light candles either for Shabbat or for Chanukah, but not both. The sage Rava responds: "It is obvious to me" that Shabbat takes precedence. Why? The reason he gives is that he sees harmony in the home as the higher priority. Shabbat candles illuminate the home, and it is deemed more important that there be light in the home for the enjoyment of Shabbat than that the festival be observed in fullness.

Here we encounter the distinction the Mussar masters drew between working on things that are entirely encompassed within our individual selves and our personal lives, which are categorized as *bein adam l'atzmo*—between a person and themselves—and the types of behaviors that are in the *bein adam l'chaveiro* category—that is, between one person and another.[6] My humility or arrogance, or my envy and judgment, only relate to me and my own inner state of affairs. In contrast, *shalom* is not a personal trait. I may want peace for myself, but my inner state will only be a reflection of and dependent upon the interpersonal relations that surround me as an individual. "Harmony in the home" is a prime example of this because no one can be truly at peace if the household is in turmoil.

The eighteenth-century sage, Rabbi Chaim Yosef David Azulai, known as the Chida,[7] warns us to be careful to welcome Shabbat with *shalom* and not with squabbling. It is a well-known phenomenon that when we get very busy with a deadline looming, as happens every Friday afternoon when all the preparations for Shabbat need to be completed, it is not only the temperature of the chicken that rises. The pressure brought on by the approach of Shabbat can bring tension and discord into the home.

The way the Chida puts it, on Friday evening, the unwelcome guest known as Satan comes into our homes with the mission of creating anger and tension. His words reflect the time and place he lived in, but convey a universal truth:

> [Friday afternoon] is a dangerous time for conflict between husband and wife and with the servants, as the Satan increases its efforts to instigate quarreling. The God-fearing person will subdue his evil inclination so there will be no disagreement or insistence on having one's way. To the contrary, one should pursue peace.

Here, the Chida refers to the instigator of conflict as the Satan, but regardless of the terminology, we are going to be very familiar with the phenomenon: so much still needs to get done, time is short, and no one is doing it right, or fast enough, or as I would like . . . and that match inches closer and closer to the fuse until *Pow*, it ignites, and out flows a torrent of harsh and hurtful words.

That sort of behavior destroys harmony in the home and Shabbat with it. Pursuing peace requires that we be aware of the places where we have a tendency to slip into irritation and annoyance, and that we guard those junctures carefully so that we bring peace to the home and not a conflagration.

The importance of harmony in the home, along with some clues about how to achieve it, is embedded in a long and learned story[8] that I love. I don't know if there are any other people in the world that have scholarly humor, but Jews do.

A new rabbi came to town and saw that the *mikvah*—the ritual bath—was in terrible condition and needed to be rebuilt. The first step for any project like that is, of course, raising the funds, and because he was new to town, he asked others to suggest who might donate to the project.

The list of names that was presented to him was very short, and so he asked, "Is there anyone else who has been blessed with resources?"

Yes, they answered, there was one other person, but he is a hard-hearted miser and will never donate.

"Let me see what I can do," said the rabbi.

So, the rabbi went to the miser's house and knocked on the door. A man answered, saw the rabbi, and barked gruffly, "Whatever you want, I won't give it to you."

"I don't want anything," responded the rabbi. "I actually came to give you something. I came to ask if there was anything for which you might want a blessing?"

The man was a little taken aback but quickly recovered: "As a matter of fact," he said, "there is something. Could you give me a blessing that my wife should die?"

Now it was the rabbi's turn to be taken aback. "That I can't do," he said. "Blessings can only be for the good. But why would you want such a thing anyway?" asked the rabbi.

"Nothing but nagging and fighting, harsh words and nasty deeds. It is so miserable to have her around that I just wish she were dead," complained the man.

The rabbi thought quickly, "Well, I can't offer a blessing for that to happen, but there just might be something I can do. The rabbis taught that a person who begins to undertake a commandment and then fails to complete it will be punished by having his wife and children die.[9] I hate to advise you in this direction, but it might work for you. You could vow to do something, then not fulfill the vow, and expect the punishment to fall on your wife."

"That sounds wonderful," said the miser. "Just what I need." Then he thought for a moment, "But what could I vow?"

The rabbi could offer a suggestion: "Well, for example, you could vow to fund the new *mikvah* we are building, and then you simply don't fulfill the vow. That should do it."

Without a second's hesitation, the miser proclaimed, "I vow to fund the entire cost of building the new *mikvah*. And I won't give a cent!" he exclaimed.

"Very well," said the rabbi, and he departed.

A few weeks later, the rabbi dropped by and asked the miser how it was going.

"It isn't working," the man replied. "Nothing has happened."

"Hmmm," pondered the rabbi. "I wonder why that might be. Let me ask you, when your wife has insulted you, have you ever responded by insulting her back, standing by an open window or door, so someone passing by might have heard you?"

"I might have done that," said the miser. "What difference should that make?"

"Well," said the rabbi, "we are taught that someone who insults another person in public, it is as if they killed that person.[10] So, if someone heard you insult your wife, it means that you have effectively executed the retribution on her. She is technically already dead. If you want the real punishment to befall her, you have to change how you respond to her. If she insults you, you need to respond to her patiently and kindly. If she tells you that you are a boor and she hates you, thank her for the feedback. Repay her every harsh word with a kindness or even a gift. Do that and you are sure to have your wish fulfilled."

After a few weeks, the rabbi again came by to ask the miser how it was going.

This time, when the miser opened the door, he was white as a sheet and shaking so badly that he couldn't speak. "What's wrong?" asked the rabbi. "What's happened?"

"I want my vow annulled!" cried the miser. "How can I cancel my vow?"

"That's not possible," answered the rabbi. "Once the vow has been sworn, it stands in the heavenly court.[11] But why the change of heart?"

"I need that vow annulled!" cried the miser. "I followed your advice. Whenever my wife called me a name, I smiled sweetly and called her by an affectionate name. If she told me that she hated something I did, I thanked her for the feedback. When she yelled at me, I responded softly and kindly."

"At first, she didn't notice the change and just carried on berating me. But after a while, she stopped with the insults and harsh words. I kept on calling her 'dear' and 'darling,' and after a little while, she actually called me 'dear.' Soon it was 'dear me' and 'dear you' and 'darling me' and 'darling you.'"

"Now we are so in love that you have to help me annul that vow! Don't let her be taken from me! I love her so much!"

"I am afraid that there is no way to annul the vow," said the rabbi. "But there may yet be a solution. Your wife will die only if you *fail* to fulfill your vow. Now, if you should happen to fulfill the vow, then there shouldn't be any sort of punishment, should there? Would you consider fulfilling your vow?"

"Yes! Yes!" said the former miser. "Wait here. I'll go get the keys to my treasury."

The man ran off. The rabbi smiled.

Cultivating Peace

That story teaches us a lot about the essence of harmony at home. It underlines the influence our habits have over our lives, and what can happen in a relationship when we recognize those habits, take responsibility for our behavior, and change it. An especially important lesson it teaches is that the behavior we have to be most concerned about is our speech and the impact we can expect to arise from harsh words as opposed to kind words.

When we go back to the primary source for the observance of Shabbat, we find that the Torah imposes only one prohibition for the seventh day, where it says:[12]

You shall kindle no fire throughout your dwellings on the Sabbath day.

This injunction is meant to be taken literally, and the Torah goes on to relate that a person who was found gathering firewood on Shabbat was considered to have committed a very serious crime, enough to merit forfeiting their life.[13] That prohibition comes down to us in the form of avoidance of igniting or extinguishing flames or turning on or off electrical devices.

But the sacred text, the Zohar,[14] interprets this ritual enactment more broadly to mean that it is forbidden to light a fire on Shabbat "even within one's body." This means that not only are we not to burn a fire in the fireplace on Shabbat, but we are also not to allow the fire of anger to ignite within us on that holy day.

Shabbat rituals are not just a checklist of behaviors we do; they are meant to remind us to act in ways that fulfill the aspiration embedded in the ritual. And so, the rabbis ruled that even if we never turn on the stove or the coffeepot on Shabbat, even if we don't check our email or drive the car, if we still ignite the fires of bickering, we will have failed to observe Shabbat as the Torah directs, nor as a day of shalom.

Heinrich Heine captures this idea in a verse from his ode to the Sabbath[15] that personifies Shabbat as a princess who is averse to "witty warfare" and "intellectual combat":

Princess Sabbath, rest incarnate,

Held in hearty detestation

Every form of witty warfare

And of intellectual combat.

This is one of the ways that observing Shabbat becomes an exercise in building harmony in the home and, as a consequence, in our own hearts. And just to highlight the issue, the rabbis tell us that the effect of fostering harmony at home extends far beyond the home itself:

Rabban Shimon ben Gamliel would say, "Anyone who brings *shalom* into their own home is regarded by the Torah as if they had brought *shalom* to everyone in Israel."[16]

This is not just hyperbole, because is it not reasonable to say that harmony in our own homes is a contribution we can make to peace in the world?

These lessons apply not just on Shabbat but on the other six days of the week as well, and also to the cultivation of harmony in every relationship in our lives.

Harmony in the home is no small or easy matter that gets accomplished just because in a moment of peace and clarity you say, "That's it! I won't bicker anymore. From now on, the house will be a haven of peace." The truth is that it is hard work to change ourselves enough to change the dynamics in our relationships. It is, in fact, the index of all spiritual growth because our own personal spiritual curriculum shows up nowhere more clearly or more powerfully than in our interpersonal relationships, especially with people with whom we are close.

That reminds me of another story.

A person is walking along the sandy beach and happens to kick up an old brass lamp that lay buried in the sand. Wanting to see what the lamp looks like, the person brushes off all the sand and dirt and then, whoosh, a genie appears.

The genie bows low and thanks the person for freeing him from the confines of the lamp and says that, in return, he will offer to grant the person one wish.

This story took place where I live, in Vancouver, where there are many sandy beaches. And just as I myself might do, the person immediately tells the genie, "What I would like for my wish is that there would be a causeway between here and Hawaii so I could just drive there and escape winter."

"Ooooh," says the genie. "That is a very big and difficult wish. Do you perhaps have another wish that's a bit simpler that would satisfy you?"

"Well, as a matter of fact, there is something else," the person responds. "My spouse and I have not been getting along very well recently, and many harsh words have passed between us. I wish there would be *shalom bayit* in my home."

"Ooooh," says the genie. "Would you like that causeway to be one lane or two?"

No small matter, harmony at home. But nor should we shy away from the challenge. That is a consistent message our tradition gives us. And the school for harmony that they provide to us is Shabbat. Bear it in mind: light no fires, not even the fire of anger that can burn within yourself.

The goal is not to restrain ourselves from lashing out in anger by grinding our teeth and clenching our jaws. The goal is to develop mastery over our inner life so that any impulse to anger does not rule over us, but we rule over it.

We all live our lives in the inner world of our thoughts, ideals, and feelings, our aspirations and our concerns, as well as in the outer world of actions. Not infrequently, there is a great dissonance between, on the one hand, what we think about and our perception of ourselves and the hopes we harbor in our inner lives, and, on the other, the reality of what life is like for us in our day-to-day actions. Shabbat issues a call and provides an opportunity to attain harmony between our inner selves and outer lives.

This harmony reflects the great principle articulated in the Talmud that establishes that a person's inner reality and external way of being should be in harmony, not in conflict. The way the Talmud[17] puts it is that one should strive to make one's inside like one's outside—in its phrase, "*tocho k'varo.*"

It does not say that one needs to be a perfect human being both inside and out. What it recognizes is that usually, our outward behavior is more elevated than our inner thoughts and feelings because we strive to put on our best performance in the way we speak and act. The rabbis challenge us to elevate our inner selves to the level that matches our outward behavior.

When we apply that principle to our current focus, we can see that the path to harmony in our outer world begins by cultivating that quality in our inner world. This is a subject that is the focus of a lot of Mussar writing because what we are talking about here is the inner wholeness that has been stated to be the goal of Mussar practice in general.

In the Mussar perspective, the key obstacle to spiritual growth and elevation is the specific inner traits that exist in each individual's life that tend toward one extreme or another. In other words, the issues we run into as we walk a path of spiritual growth are not the result of the fact that we possess certain traits and not others; in the Mussar view, the issues arise because we trip over certain traits which are ingrained in us either in excess or in deficiency.

Each of us possesses all the inner traits—there is no one without some measure of anger, humility, envy, kindness, etc. What puts a trait on our personal spiritual curriculum is when we have a tendency to experience and enact that trait toward an extreme end of the range, whether in excess or in deficiency.

The observance of Shabbat is a great teacher about one's own personal spiritual curriculum. That's because on Shabbat we take on certain things we willingly do, and other things we avoid doing. When we make an effort to fulfill those dos and don'ts, our own personal spiritual curriculum is likely to make an appearance in our tendency to come up short, to resist, or to reject, or to rationalize. When we pay attention to what goes on in our inner lives as we set about observing Shabbat, the lessons will be much more about us in general than they are about Shabbat in particular.

And then, when we engage with that curriculum and endeavor to develop ourselves in the way that one does when working on any curriculum, we will find ourselves becoming more whole in an ongoing way, which makes us more able to enjoy the fruits of that growth on Shabbat and all week long as well.

As we learned earlier from the Abarbanel, "when things are in their proper order, *shalom* will reign," and this is as true about the reality of our inner lives as it is about the ordering of the environment in which we live.

Getting Peaceful

It is a Mussar principle that any issue of the inner life should be addressed in small steps. We can enact that principle in our pursuit of harmony on Shabbat by committing to refrain from arguing or harsh words for a specified period of time. You can decide whether the defined period is five minutes or fifteen minutes or some other length of time, as long as you choose a duration that is both a bit of a stretch for you and still very attainable. Being overambitious in Mussar practice tends to lead to setbacks more than breakthroughs.

Record in your journal whatever experiences you had as you made efforts to bring more peace and harmony into your Shabbat.

Were you able to do it? What effect did it have on how you experienced Shabbat? What about your relationships with the people with whom you did (or did not) exchange arguments or harsh words? What conclusions do you draw?

Reflect on which inner traits showed up as you made an effort to create more wholeness and harmony in your world—both inner and outer—on Shabbat. Upon further reflection, you will likely be able to see that issues with those same *middot* show up not only on Shabbat but throughout your life.

6

Silence

Blessed Silence

One of the only words I remember from my pre-bar mitzvah Hebrew school days is *sheket*, and that is because it was the word I heard most in those years. No matter what subject we were studying, our teachers were constantly shouting at us unruly and noisy kids to "*Sheket*"—Be quiet!!

Many of us want to yell something like that at the whole world. We live in such an unceasingly noisy environment! City dwellers—and that is the majority of us these days—are regularly exposed to noise above 85 decibels[1] from traffic, sirens, construction, trains, industrial activity, airports, and airplanes. That's higher than the 80-decibel noise level produced by an alarm clock. The level of urban noise is high enough to cause significant hearing loss over time.

Even if you retreat deep into a forest, there is a good chance the silence will be interrupted by the drone of an airplane or the drumming of a helicopter overhead. Your ears easily pick up the distant roar of a passing freeway or music blaring from someone else's campsite.

As we begin our look into silence, I confess that I am a bit hesitant to start pouring out a river of words in explanation. Silence speaks best for the value of silence. There is a cautionary tale along these lines in the sixteenth-century Mussar text, *Orchot Tzaddikim*,[2] that tells of two advocates who stood before the king, one to argue that speech is best and the other to make the case for silence being superior.

The one who spoke on behalf of speech argued the point eloquently, and the king said, "You have spoken well!" When the other rose to praise silence, as soon as he began to speak, the first advocate interrupted him.

The king asked, "Why did you interrupt him?" He said, "My Lord, I taught from what is mine concerning what is mine, for I taught the value of speech by speaking. He is using my means—speech—to praise silence."

The advocate of silence said to him, "Solomon[3] did not say that God wants you to sit silent as a mute. But he did say, 'In the multitude of words there is no lack of transgression; and one who restrains one's lips is wise.'"[4]

He makes an important point. The category of silence includes not only the type of quiet where not a sound is registered but also the tempering of our verbosity.

It's unclear which of these Elie Wiesel had in mind when he responded to an interviewer[5] who asked him if there was silence in Jewish practice. Wiesel replied: "Judaism is full of silences . . . but we don't talk about them."

So please forgive me for employing words to explore silence. Silence itself is indeed a great teacher, as we learn from the sage Rabban Shimon ben Gamliel, who is quoted as saying:[6]

All my days I have grown up among the wise, and I have found nothing better for the body than silence.

But, alas, there is still a need for words so we can learn what our teachers have to say on this subject.

Mind Your Tongue

As I mentioned, the *middah* of silence has two aspects. The first is the one to which the advocate who argued on behalf of silence in *Orchot Tzaddikim* alluded in quoting Proverbs—"In the multitude of words there is no lack of transgression; and one who restrains one's lips is wise"—which brings us to the subject of restraint in speaking.

Elsewhere in that same book of the Bible, it ups the ante by saying, "Death and life are in the power of the tongue."[7]

And just in case that didn't hit hard enough, Proverbs includes yet another incisive comment on this subject, saying, "One who guards their mouth and tongue protects their soul from trouble."[8]

The focus here is on what is called in Hebrew *shmirat ha'lashon,* a term that literally means, "guarding the tongue." The Hebrew poet of twelfth-century Spain, Yosef Kimchi, makes the argument from anatomy:[9]

You have but one tongue—
never a pair in its cave:
and two high walls surround it,
with teeth and lips arrayed;
therefore twice consider
all that you might say—
and treat your tongue as a treasure
to guard till your dying day.

The teachings in Jewish sources about this topic encourage us to take steps to ensure that our speech has a positive, and not a negative, impact. Or, to quote Kimchi again:

The less said, the fewer mistakes;
the greater the talk, the greater the headache.

It is hard to argue with the sentiment, but even harder to learn to hold yourself back from uttering unnecessary and especially potentially damaging speech. It is a Mussar practice simply to keep your mouth shut at certain times because words are powerful, and sometimes the best thing you can do for all concerned is simply to refrain from speaking.

Rabbi Abraham Isaac Kook, who among other distinctions was the first Ashkenazi Chief Rabbi of Israel, makes this point very simply and directly, saying: "One kind of silence means stopping speech."[10]

Communication is a wonderful thing, but we also know that words can do much harm. Rav Kook is here pointing out the importance of taking control of what we say and do not say so our words will be as positive as possible. Sometimes, that means having the strength to say nothing at all.

Rabbi Israel Meir Kagan, who was known as the Chofetz Chaim, a great sage of the early twentieth century, wrote an entire book on the topic entitled *Shmirat Ha'Lashon* in which he identifies thirty-one commandments that can be violated when a person speaks or even listens to speech that harms another person in some way. He emphasized how important it is to be very careful to choose what we say, and also what we do not say.

Orchot Tzaddikim, that I referred to earlier, makes this point explicitly, writing, "Just as there is a time to open and a time to close the door of a house, so should one close the doors of one's mouth. Just as you would guard silver, gold and pearls in your room, within a case, making one enclosure within another, do the same with your mouth."

These injunctions stand on the foundation of the tremendous respect that exists in Judaism for the power of words. Remember that in the story of the creation of the world itself, God brought everything into being only with words.[11] "And God *said,* let there be . . . and it was." In the daily prayers, a prominent one, the one that begins the second section of the morning service, opens with the words "*Baruch she'amar*"—which calls on us to "bless the One who spoke."[12]

And it is not only the words uttered by God that are seen to be powerful. In translating the Torah's story of the creation of Adam into Aramaic, the translator Onkelos renders the words "and Adam became a living soul"[13] as "and Adam became a speaking spirit."[14] In this deep realm of Jewish thought, speech is the defining feature of humanity itself.

Because Judaism holds speech to be so fundamental and so powerful, our ancestors gave careful attention to drawing the line between the sorts of speech that are creative and beneficial and the kinds of speech that can do harm, and they obligated us to opt for the former. Think of it as an ancestral form of gun control, only the hardware is mouth and tongue.

In establishing what Jewish law considers to be "right" speech and differentiating it from speech that ought not be spoken, you might expect that the rabbis would pay a great deal of attention to the issue of whether the spoken words are true, but that is not the case. Their primary focus is on whether the impact of our words will do good or cause harm.

Blessings, prayer, kindness, and compassion uttered through speech contribute to building a holy world. And at the other end of the scale, the Talmud tells us that "Evil speech kills three people: the person speaking, the person spoken to, and the person being spoken about."[15]

This subject is hugely important today because never before in human history have there been so many ways to share our words, and with ease to send them far and wide. We have the ability to speak directly, phone someone, send a text, post to social media, email, tweet, publish, and more. Our great-grandparents would consider FaceTime or WhatsApp pure magic.

These many ways of communicating bear with them in equal measure opportunity, danger, and responsibility. Imagine if everyone applied the Jewish practice of guarding the tongue to all of their speech—in person, in writing, in the media, online, in politics, etc. How different our world would be!

Of course, as our interlocutor from *Orchot Tzaddikim* protested, this issue cannot be addressed by just keeping your lips permanently zipped because there are also times when speech is called for and much needed. These are times when your voice ought to be heard, and one nineteenth-century Mussar source, *Pele Yoetz*,[16] quotes the Zohar as saying that there is a punishment for speaking negatively, but there is also a punishment for not speaking up when your words could have done good.

Therefore, what becomes clear is that the real practice in this area is not actually silence itself but rather *discernment*, which means having a clear sense of when to speak, what to say, and when to hold your peace.

This is the guideline we find in Ecclesiastes (3:17), in the famous passage that tells us that there is a time to keep silent and a time to speak.

That notion is echoed in the Talmud (Zevachim 115b), where it mirrors the Zohar in saying that there are "times that one is silent and receives reward for the silence, and at times one speaks and receives reward for the speech."

And of course, what is tricky for us is knowing which is which, and having the inner strength to carry that discernment through into action.

It is a sad fact that, in general, most of us speak out our thoughts as soon as they come into our heads. Our words fly out of our mouths before the mind has had a chance to give even a split-second's reflection on what is about to be said. The Mussar masters urge us to break into that automatic, unreflective use of the power of speech by adopting the simple (though that is not to say, easy) intervention of pausing for a second or two before speaking.

Usually, what prompts us to speak before we think—ready, fire, aim, as I have heard it described—is emotion. Angry, insulted, worried, fearful, provoked—out flies our counterattack. If we can inject even a moment or two of silence before speaking, we create a space in which to collect ourselves, to give ourselves a chance to become more aware of our feelings and the motives that are influencing what we are about to say, and to create a more mindful place from which to communicate in a more responsible way that is congruent with our deeper values and aspirations. Or to say that more simply, taking a pause before speaking will usually result in much less regret.

This is the advice the *Pele Yoetz* gives, putting it, "judgment should precede every speech, whether it is proper to speak or good to cease."

We find that many Mussar sources recommend inserting a silent pause, especially before answering back to something that provokes an emotional response in us, and nothing more than anger. As I mentioned above, my Mussar teacher, Rabbi Yechiel Yitzchok Perr, speaks of Mussar practice helping to open "a space between the match and the fuse." Pausing before reacting affords us a better perspective from which to respond and holds out the possibility that we will not spew out words before we even think about what we are about to say—words we later regret.

Had Derek Bentley taken that moment's pause before speaking, he might have spared his life. Bentley was a petty criminal, only sixteen years of age in 1952, when he and his friend, Craig, attempted to rob a warehouse. The friend carried a gun, and when neighbors called the police, a confrontation ensued. A police officer ordered Craig, "Hand over the gun," and Bentley shouted, "Let him have it, Craig." In response, Craig fired, killing the police officer.

If Bentley had paused to think before speaking, he might have realized that "Let him have it" can be taken two ways. At his trial, the defense argued that Bentley was cooperating with the police and telling Craig to hand over his weapon. The jury did not buy that argument, however, and Bentley was hanged.

By taking a pause before speaking, we give ourselves the possibility of making a choice about what we say, and that is important because, in addition to speech, free will is another key defining feature of being human. Only humans have the capacity to freely choose their response, as distinct from animals, who respond instinctively. But even we human beings can be animal-like in our response to provocation when we blurt out words without thinking and making a choice about what we want to say.

Jewish sources offer many techniques to open up that space between the match and the fuse. There was a Chassidic leader who would dispense "holy water" that was guaranteed to eliminate all domestic conflicts. Whenever a husband or wife had an urge to argue, he or she was instructed to hold some of this special water in his or her mouth without swallowing for as long as possible. Not surprisingly, this "holy water" proved to be very effective in stopping arguments and defusing anger.

Similarly, the Mussar teacher, the Alter of Kelm, made a personal resolution never to get angry unless he first put on a special garment he had set aside as his "anger clothes." This, too, was a practical technique that had the effect of introducing a pause between the stimulus and the response—to open a moment of silence between what he experienced as provocation and his response.

In the nineteenth-century Mussar book, *Cheshbon HaNefesh*, the chapter on silence opens with the injunction:

Before you open your mouth, be silent and reflect: "What benefit will my speech bring to me or others?"

This is the key. Jewish guidance highlights the importance of silence as a fence we can install around our speech to prevent our mouths from uttering harmful words. It is a fence, but not a wall, because we still want to be able to engage in the positive dimensions of speech. As I said earlier, the practice in this area is not a blanket directive to clamp shut our jaws but rather to develop clarity of discernment as to the impact our speech will have in the world, and then to cultivate the strength that will allow us to speak in ways that foster positive outcomes, whether that means speaking up or holding silence.

Contemplative Silence

A second concept of silence refers to inner quiet, which I have described elsewhere as "to be inwardly still. . ., to abide in a suspended state of receptive reverence."[17]

Writing in the thirteenth century, the Jewish poet of Provencal, Rabbi Avraham Bedersi, considered the Hebrew word *sheket*, which in its simple meaning denotes "silence," and concluded that it is a more intense form of *shalom*, peace.[18] While *sheket* literally means "silence," Rabbi Bedersi finds in this word a sense of not just an absence of sound, but a quieting of the stress and toil that forces people to be in constant motion. In other words, while *shalom* means "peace," *sheket* has the connotation of "stillness."

It is only by cultivating an inner stillness that we can get in touch with our deeper selves. There is so much to hear if we develop the ability to listen and reflect at that deeper level. But we can only get to hear those deep messages once the chatter stops.

Earlier I quoted Rav Kook, who identified guarding our tongues as a form of silence. Rav Kook also points to this form of inner quiet, saying: "This type of silence arrives together with the most hidden, beautiful and exalted thought."

Contemplative silence has long had a place in Jewish practice. There are traditions of day-long silences, which are named by terms that relate to fasting: "*tzom shtikah*" or "*ta'anit dibbur*." The first translates as a "fast of silence," and the second a "fast from speech."

When I first began reading about Mussar, I came across a story about Rabbi Yosef Yozel Hurwitz (1847–1919), known as the Alter of the Novardok school of Mussar. The Alter lived a typically worldly life as a businessman and householder until he had a mid-life spiritual awakening. After his wife's death, Hurwitz divided his children among relatives and retreated to a room attached to the home of a benefactor. He remained in that room for a year and a half without emerging. To guarantee his solitude, he blocked the entrance to his quarters with a brick wall, which contained two small windows. Dairy meals came through one window, and meat through the other.

When I first encountered this bit of Mussar history, I was amazed and inspired by the depth of his commitment to his spiritual life. No rabbi I had met lived with that degree of devotion and self-sacrifice. And he did it in order to seek the divine without distraction, to enter silence in order to connect.

The Alter was practicing what is known in Hebrew as *hitbodedut*, which means "self-seclusion." He sought silent seclusion in order to connect to God because, as the Torah says (1 Kings 19:11-12): "God is not in the whirlwind. God is not in the earthquake. God is not in the fire. God is in the *kol d'mama dakah*"—a still, small voice that can only be heard within the inner stillness.

The psalm[19] says it clearly: "Be still, and know that I am God."

When we enter a state of inner quiet, we make it possible to hear and encounter what is otherwise inaccessible to us. A rabbinic teaching tells us that when God gave the Torah, it was into a world that was perfectly silent:[20]

> Said Rabbi Abbahu in the name of Rabbi Yochanan: "When the Holy One gave the Torah, no bird screeched, no bird flew, no ox bellowed, none of the angels flapped a wing, nor did the celestial beings chant 'Holy, Holy, Holy!' The sea did not roar, and none of the creatures uttered a sound. Throughout the entire world there was only a deafening silence as the Divine Voice went forth speaking: 'I am the Lord your God.'"

Only when we are silent can we hear the voice of God. Everything else needs to be silent in order for the heavenly message to be heard.

This is put so beautifully in Psalm 19, which begins:

> The heavens declare the glory of God
> The skies proclaim the work of His hands.
> Day to day they pour forth speech,
> Night to night they communicate knowledge.
> There is no speech, there are no words,
> Their voice is not heard.
> Yet their music carries throughout the earth.

The psalm begins by pointing to all the divine messages that are pouring forth: "The heavens declare . . . the skies proclaim . . . day to day they pour forth speech." This part of the psalm presents four verbs and six nouns that reference speech. Incline a quieted ear toward the world, it says, and you will hear existence itself proclaiming the glory of that which is beyond the human, beyond nature, beyond space and time.

But then it reverses and informs us that "There is no speech, there are no words, their voice is not heard."

Don't take me literally, says the psalm. I am not talking about ordinary speech, the utterance of human words. The messages sent by the heavens and the skies are proclaimed wordlessly, in silence, into the stillness.

And yet, despite communicating in silence, "their music carries throughout the earth."

There is much that is real in the world, and only some of it can be captured in the small boxes we call words. There are many profound messages that are equally real and that we are capable of perceiving and understanding that cannot be communicated in or by words. To hear these messages, we need to calm the deluge of words that flows within. The still, small voice cannot be heard over the roar of the rapids, but when the deep waters flow silently, many truths can be heard that are otherwise drowned out.

Rav Kook points out that silence makes it possible to hear thoughts that cannot be heard in a cluttered, noisy mind, which he calls "the most hidden, beautiful and exalted thought." My own Mussar teacher, Rabbi Perr, said something similar. "If you are never silent," he said, "you will never be able to hear the thoughts that come to you *min ha'Shamayim*—from heaven."

This is the sort of silence that the Maharal of Prague, Rabbi Yehudah Loew (1512–1609), had in mind when he explains[21] that speech is a physical act, but when we are silent, the spiritual takes over.

Silent Shabbat

Silence on Shabbat, of both types, is set against the fact that our modern lives—outer and inner—are filled with ceaseless chatter and clatter from so many sources! This is part of the appeal of carving out a period of quiet for ourselves. Shabbat observance calls on us to put down the electronic devices, to separate from the newsfeeds, to disconnect from social media, to stay away from the car. And when we do those things, many of the major sources of racket in our lives are stilled, and space opens into which silence can seep.

Disconnecting is sure to quiet our lives in some ways, but it remains true that Shabbat is generally a time for gathering, communal prayer, singing, family meals, and the like, none of which is done silently. But, in fact, silence is one of the primary traits of Shabbat. It figures prominently in the list of things that are mentioned in the Shabbat afternoon prayer service, where we pray for "a rest of love and generosity, a rest of truth and faith, a rest of harmony, serenity, silence and trust." Silence—there it is; and on Shabbat it is that important.

Silence earned its place in the Shabbat liturgy because of the role it played in the creation story itself. The rabbinic text, *Chapters of First Principles* (5:1),[22] tells us that God created the world with Ten Utterances, the final one of which was to create the human. That happened on the sixth day of creation, and it was only later, on the seventh day, that God "rested" from creating the world and in the process, created *menucha* [rest] itself. This implies that rest was not part of the corpus of Utterances with which God created the world, which ended with the creation of the human on the sixth day. Not being uttered, rest must have been created from a silence when God did not speak. Silence itself is therefore the root source from which *menucha* springs.

King David writes in Psalm 23 that by the side of tranquil waters— *mei menuchot*—his soul is restored. This is what stillness can do. No sound, no movement, just the present moment, and the contracted and compressed soul stretches out and is renewed.

On weekdays, the waters through which we push are anything but tranquil. We thrash through the waves because there is always so much to get done and so little time! And the sand in the hourglass is running down. Shabbat disrupts the compulsions driven by time and desire. We are invited to step away from the grunting effort and into stillness, a small pocket of eternity that breaks into the unremitting pressures that rule our lives. The stillness gives us a glimpse of ourselves and the universe beyond the temporal. It is pregnant with truth, revelation, insight, and wisdom.

Considering how we spend our time day in and day out, the very concept of a day of stillness and quiet is disruptive. Shabbat invites you to let go of what has been, which has already become something, and also to let go of what will be, which is at this moment still nothing, so you can enter a place of stillness, the sanctified moment that is the present.

This stillness is a source of rest. The silent soul is the soul at rest. But we have learned that we are not being asked to be mute all of Shabbat. Talking and singing are part of this day as well, and when we step out of stillness and into the world of speech, we need to be careful to guard our ease by guarding our tongues.

In our consideration of the topic of *shalom*, I mentioned that the Zohar interprets the Shabbat prohibition on lighting a fire to mean that it is forbidden to light a fire on Shabbat, "even in one's body," which refers to getting angry. And indeed, we do find that it is an explicit rule on Shabbat not to engage in any arguments. And not just arguments: Jewish law says that on Shabbat, one should not speak about anything that might cause another person sadness or pain. Consequently, the guideline is not to share any news that could cause sadness or aggravation to another person.

Think about what this practice requires. We not only have to pause before we speak, but we also have to consider the impact our words will have on someone else. We are being called to be sensitive to how our speech will make someone else feel, and then to make the choice to avoid words that will have certain predictable impacts. This is true inner training, and Shabbat is the focus.

It makes sense that these warnings about emotions, harsh words, and conflict are issued in regard to the one day of the week when we are enjoined to pursue peace and rest. Our efforts to be peaceful, calm, gentle, and restful are a custom-made invitation to the subversive inclination that lives within all of us—what is called in Hebrew the *yetzer ha'ra*, the negative formation—to provoke us to fail, at which point we will abandon our spiritually motivated and elevated aspirations. How does that inner adversary do this? By feeding the fires of anger and impatience and goading us to speak harshly to the people in our household. Striving for peace and rest, we find ourselves diverted into anger and conflict.

From this perspective, erecting a fence around our speech protects the pleasure, harmony, and rest that are the ideals we reach for on Shabbat.

Rabbi Matisyahu Salomon,[23] the late Mussar supervisor of the Lakewood Yeshiva in New Jersey, viewed this situation from a positive perspective.[24] He said that when we work at it and actually succeed in overcoming the instigation to speak sharply to others on Friday afternoon, we will have passed a test, and that is precisely what we need to do in order to bring ourselves to the state of mind for entering Shabbat, now ready to engage with pleasure, peace, and rest.

Growing Quiet

The two dimensions of silence—careful use of the tongue and the practice of inner stillness—are both well suited to the ethos of Shabbat. After all, on the seventh day of creation, God not only stopped creating, but God stopped talking, too. Every day of the six days of creation, God speaks in order to create, but on the seventh day, God stops *both* speaking and creating.

By observing positive speech on Shabbat, we can develop heightened awareness of our inner impulses. Based on that awareness, we can get better at opening up a space between those impulses and our words and actions. This training gives us the possibility of acting from free will to bring our words and deeds into alignment with the highest aspirations we hold for ourselves, rather than just snapping and growling like animals that are guided only by primitive instincts.

And since every Friday afternoon is harried and pressured, this is a recurring challenge. As we face it week after week, we are giving ourselves training in awareness and a workout in the process of developing the capacity to overcome anger and to confront challenging situations without lashing out with weaponized words. Engaging with our instinctive responses in this way is training in how to lift them—and us—to a higher level and thus to grow, seven days a week.

A parallel opportunity to grow through Shabbat practice presents itself regarding contemplative silence. Shabbat is already a day we call holy, and what I want to bring into focus here is what we can do to instill that holiness in our inner lives. To paraphrase the Maharal, by opening up periods of silence on Shabbat, we prepare ourselves to touch and experience the holy within.

Silence on Shabbat evokes the spirit of rest that divinity instilled on the seventh day. When we make silence part of our Shabbat, we are emulating God, walking in God's way. Earlier I quoted Rabban Shimon ben Gamliel from *Pirkei Avot* (1:17), saying that silence is good for the body. And if that is true for the body, how much more so for the mind and spirit!

It takes practice to get good at being silent and guarding your tongue. Here are practices that will help you develop both capacities:

a. Guarding the Tongue

At the nineteenth-century Mussar yeshiva in Kelm, they had a practice of contemplating actively before any conversation with the goal of seeking to discern what God wanted them to say. This historical Mussar practice suggests something we can do as well.

Assign yourself the practice of pausing before you speak to ask yourself a question such as: "What does God want me to say?" or it could be, "Will my words do good and not harm?" The question you ask yourself needs to be fitting to you, and, in fact, the question is less important than the practice of opening up the space before speaking in which to consider in advance what you are thinking to say, and to evaluate its impact.

b. Contemplative Silence

A fully silent Shabbat is a contradiction, but a Shabbat without silence is a lost opportunity. I recommend that you identify in advance a short period on Shabbat when it will be possible for you to seek out and accept silence. It could be as short as ten or fifteen undisturbed minutes at any point between Friday and Saturday evenings.

When you enter this period of silence that you have set aside, invite yourself to be fully present in the moment without distraction. Bring the flow of thoughts and concerns to a halt and allow stillness to permeate your mind. As you settle into that uncluttered, receptive inner state, listen to the messages that come to you in the silence, remembering that you cannot expect to hear these messages in the form of ordinary speech. As the psalm says:

There is no speech, there are no words,
Their voice is not heard.
Yet their music carries throughout the earth.

As for your journal practice, after Shabbat, record your experience in your journal. You can also use your journal to summarize some intentions you set for yourself regarding the soul-trait of silence.

Also, in your journaling, consider one or the other or both of the dimensions of silence we have just reviewed:

- Are there areas of your life in which you could practice more restraint in speech? Do you have a tendency to gossip? Or is there a context where you are regularly exposed to damaging speech? Is there a relationship where you tend to say too much, and it does not work toward the good? Consider these and other possibilities that apply to you, and then set down your intention to restrain your speech or your exposure to the speech of others, and then use your journal to record your experiences in this area.

- The Mussar teachers, as the Talmudic sages before them, roundly praised the practice of contemplative silence, whether in meditation, contemplation, or just being quiet and in retreat. Is that sort of silence already part of your regular routine? If not, would you set an intention to spend more quiet time? What form would you see that taking?

When we undertake to bring silence into our lives in these ways, we can become masters of silence, and while that may be something we practice and learn on Shabbat, the dividend is the ability to be masters of our tongues and people who know stillness whenever the needs of the moment or of the spirit call for us to be quiet, 365 days a year.

7

Trust¹

You can get out of bed in the morning, eat breakfast, and tackle whatever it is that is on your agenda for the day because you trust. You trust that the sun will come up and the day will begin. You trust that the food is safe and that the world will respond to your efforts in predictable ways. You trust that when you press the button, the device will respond. You trust that you have enough time to do what you set out to do.

None of that may turn out to be true, of course, but stepping into and through daily activities is based on the inner trait of trust, and the more you trust, the more confident you will be in doing whatever it is you do.

How much more so does putting down all your worldly activities on Friday evening demand trust because, without some sense that things will work out, you'd never be able to let go of the anxieties, desires, hopes, and fears that drive your weekday activities.

The trust we have begun to explore here is called *bitachon* in Hebrew, and in the Mussar world, there is no ambiguity: *bitachon* means "trust in God." That's what makes it both a very challenging trait and an essential factor that allows us to set down our worldly burdens on Friday evening. This sort of trust is also something that can have an enormous positive impact on our lives, and we are cautioned: "It is better to trust in God than to trust in any person" (Psalm 118:9).

Trust is related to, though not the same thing as, faith [*emunah*, in Hebrew]. Faith encompasses your conviction that there is a superarching divine force at work in the universe. It's a second step to say that you trust this divinity to be a force for good in the universe and in your life. A metaphor I like to use to explain the difference is that *emunah* means that you recognize there is a wall, whereas *bitachon* means shifting your center of gravity to lean on it. That's where trust comes in.

This is a challenging trait for almost everyone, and part of the challenge lies in the abundant evidence that trusting God does not necessarily deliver the outcome you think would be best for you in your life. Look at all the terrible things that happen to good and innocent people. So why should anyone trust God?

Reflecting on the fact that to this day American bills and coins proclaim the message, "In God We Trust," Rabbi Yaakov Yosef Herman once said:[2] "America exists in the merit of the penny."

But what does it actually mean to say, "In God We Trust"? As we delve into Mussar thought on that question, we find a wide range of understandings of the concept and the reality presented by different Mussar teachers. A key difference among the teachings is the question of how much effort we are required or responsible to put in on our own behalf and at what point we ought to stop making an effort and hand the whole thing over to God to work out.

At one extreme, we find the camp of Rabbi Yosef Yozel Hurwitz, the founder of the Novardok school of Mussar, and hence known as the Alter of Novardok. The Alter held that a person needs to do nothing at all, and God will provide everything.

From that school of thought, the spectrum stretches right across to others who say that we are absolutely obligated to make significant efforts on our own behalf and to use whatever natural means we can employ to pursue our goals, or else we can't expect God to take up our cause. Rabbi Yerucham Levovitz, the revered spiritual supervisor of the Mir yeshiva in pre-war Belarus, quotes the medieval commentator, the Ramban, who wrote that the Torah expounded at length each and every detail regarding the gifts that Jacob sent to appease his brother Esau in order to show that Jacob "made effort to succeed [in saving himself] to the best of his ability."[3]

Between those poles, we find others who say that we are required to make some effort, but they see our actions as a necessary token or symbolic gesture. We are obligated to do something, though what we do won't have any role in bringing about the outcome, which remains entirely in the hands of God. This is the view of the relatively modern and influential sage known as the Chazon Ish,[4] who wrote that trust "is the belief that nothing happens by chance, and that everything that occurs under the sun is the result of a decree of God." God wants us to make an effort as we see best, but we need to trust that it is God who decrees whether or not the deal will go through, or the illness will be cured.

All along the spectrum, we find that different teachers identify different points at which they say the right thing to do is to cease making an effort and, instead, turn over our burden to God. In fact, these differences are not just about definitions; the very nature of the trust that is being asked of us has a different character and substance at various points along the continuum.

These varied approaches reflect differing notions of God's role in the world and in our lives. All of them have traditional and modern sources that support them, and all have been adopted by groups or individuals in the Jewish community over time. No one can lay claim to the objective and universal truth about the nature of trust, however. What we have here is a variety of viewpoints, any one of which will be more appropriate to a certain individual at a certain time in their life, according to the personal spiritual matrix through which they interact with the world at that moment. I want to outline four such refractions on trust that apply to observing Shabbat and that can have a deep impact on the people we become and how we lead our lives. Your task is to decide which one most applies to you.

Refractions of Trust

Refraction #1: Trust as Resignation

It is Friday afternoon and I'm all tied up in an activity, maybe even dealing with a crisis, and there is a lot at stake. But daylight is fading, and there is nothing I can do about that. Loose ends, even major ones, are hanging. Because I am committed to ceasing all secular activities with the ending of the day, there is actually nothing I can do about the issues. So, I might as well relax and trust God.

Under these circumstances, there is just no point in fruitless worrying. Or, as the Talmud puts it,[5] "Do not suffer from tomorrow's trouble, as you do not know what the day will bring."

We can hear this sort of trust in a story about what happened to a man named Yisroel, whose business involved selling on the Amazon platform.[6] One Friday, just twenty minutes before sundown, Yisroel received notice that his Amazon account had been suspended for suspected manipulation of reviews after he sent a message to customers asking them how his company could earn their five-star review. "In these cases, Amazon closes down the account entirely for an indeterminate amount of time. With no time before Sabbath to manage the crisis, Yisroel did the only thing he could—got dressed and went to synagogue to welcome the Sabbath."

"I tried my best not to think about it," he said. "And you know, it was a beautiful Sabbath that week."

In the three days until his account with Amazon was reinstated, he had lost $70,000 in sales. But he evinced the kind of trust that is based on resignation, saying: "Everything is always decided, that's our belief."

This type of trust reflects submission. Shabbat comes, and what will be will be and there is nothing you can do about it anyway. So don't sweat it. Put down your work.

A student of mine who runs a delicatessen told a story about what happened to him one Shabbat. It was 3 p.m. on Friday, a good two hours before the candles were to be lit. He had arrived home with enough time to help prepare Shabbat dinner and food for the day.

All was ready, and he was just about to hop into the shower when the phone rang. Work was calling in a panic because the smoked fish delivery from New York had not arrived. They faced the prospect that on Sunday, hordes of bagel-and-lox-craving customers would be disappointed. Under these circumstances, normally he would have put the goodwill of the business first and gone into the office to work the phones to solve the problem.

As his plan of action swirled in his head, he realized that he was facing a test, and he remembered *bitachon*. Would life go on if I didn't spring into action, he asked? Yes. What would happen if I did go in to solve the problem? Shabbat would be spoiled.

And so, he responded to the caller that at this late hour there was nothing he could do. They would simply have to live with the hand they were dealt and hope that all would work out. He ended the call feeling calm and trusting that—even if it didn't seem to suit him—everything was exactly as it should be.

He reported that Shabbat was particularly fulfilling that week, with lively conversation at the table and everyone deeply in the spirit. It was as if everyone at the table could sense the heightened level of trust, and that gave them the ease to be vulnerable and take risks.

He reported, "Fast forward to Sunday, it was a miracle. . . the existing supplies of smoked fish turned out to be sufficient for the entire day. Sunday brunch was saved. And so was Shabbat." And all along, he trusted—not that things would work out as he wanted, but as they should, according to a plan to which he was not privy.

Refraction #2: God Will Take Care of It

Another refraction of trust reflects the view that God takes an interest in our lives and will do what we ask. In this case, the word *bitachon* might better be translated as "reliance," which is also accurate to Hebrew. The roots of this sort of trust can be found right in the Psalms themselves.

For example, in Psalm 71:1, we read: "In You, O Lord, I have taken refuge; let me never be put to shame." The *Yalkut Shimoni*, a rabbinic commentary to the Torah compiled between the eleventh and fourteenth centuries, interprets this verse to mean:[7] "We see from here that whoever trusts in God will be saved."

Similarly, in Psalm. 32:10 we find: "Many are the sorrows of the wicked, but one who trusts in God will be surrounded by mercy." Again, the same *Yalkut Shimoni* comments on the verse:[8] "Even an evildoer who trusts in the Lord will be surrounded by mercy."

This refraction on trust became normative in some Mussar circles. As an example, the influential twentieth-century Mussar teacher, Rabbi Yechezkel Levenstein,[9] says[10] that someone with strong trust should be at this level: "Even during his trouble he should already feel he has been saved."

He could have been building on the ideas expressed by R' Yosef Zundel, who was the Mussar teacher of Rabbi Yisrael Salanter and hence the godfather of the nineteenth-century Mussar movement in eastern Europe, who said: "This is the secret of trust: that God performs the will of the person who trusts in God with a full heart and provides that person with all his needs in every place and every time."[11]

The Alter of Novardok stressed the importance of trusting wholeheartedly. He said: "A person who tries to practice trust in God while leaving himself a backup plan is like a person who tries to learn how to swim but insists on keeping one foot on the ground."

There are many stories that reveal that the Alter fulfilled his own model in action. One such story is told about a Saturday evening in Kiev at the height of the Russian Civil War, when the Alter stood to make *havdalah* to mark the end of Shabbat, and bullets suddenly came whizzing overhead. Everyone hit the floor—except the Alter. It is reported that he stood there calmly, waiting for the tempest to subside, not spilling a drop from the wine cup. His *bitachon* was such that he was completely unmoved by the smashing glass and bullets piercing the walls. And he was not hurt.

Rabbi Perr told me a story about one of the many followers of Novardok Mussar who, like his own father-in-law, in the 1940s was exiled to hard labor in Siberia. This Novardoker was so imbued with *bitachon* that he was completely indifferent to the threats of the guards and their methods of intimidation. He sang to himself and carried on in complete trust that God would certainly not allow anyone to harm him. When the guards saw his behavior, they concluded that he was out of his mind—and proceeded to leave him alone. From his perspective, his *bitachon* had been completely vindicated.

This type of *bitachon* involves trusting that God will take care of the problem in the way that the person would hope. In this view, the key to *bitachon* is to believe it. If you wholeheartedly trust that God will take care of your problem, and hence take care of you, then God will respond according to your will. The trick, of course, is to be so wholehearted in your trust, but that is what this type of *bitachon* depends upon. As the medieval Jewish philosopher, Rabbi Yosef Albo,[12] says:

> One who does not trust completely that he will be given what is in his heart, whatever he will ask, because he does not view himself as being on the spiritual level that God should do him kindness; he thinks that God does not want to grant his request, and because of this he does not hope properly. However, if he had hoped properly, the kindness will not have been withheld by God.

Refraction #3: God Does Good

Here, a person holds in their heart the conviction that what happens is what is supposed to happen and conforms to God's will, even if it turns out to be not what I think I want and need. God is inherently good and knows better than I do and so, to quote Rabbi Akiva in the Talmud,[13] "Everything that God does, God does for the best."

That statement is the central idea in a story that the Talmud tells about Rabbi Akiva himself. It relates that:

> Rabbi Akiva was walking along the road and came to a certain city. He inquired about lodging and they did not give him any. He said: "Everything that God does, God does for the best." He went and slept in a field, and he had with him a rooster, a donkey and a candle. A gust of wind came and extinguished the candle; a cat came and ate the rooster; and a lion came and ate the donkey. He said: "Everything that God does, God does for the best." That night, an army came and took the city into captivity. Rabbi Akiva alone [who was not in the city and had no lit candle, noisy rooster or donkey to give away his location], was saved. He said to them: "Didn't I tell you? Everything that God does, God does for the best."

From one perspective, Rabbi Akiva got lucky due to a happy coincidence. But that is not his perspective. He sees and teaches that everything that happens is a feature of the will of God, and everything that God does is for the best, even if it means having to sleep in a field and losing everything you have.

This is what makes this sort of *bitachon* more challenging—it is comforting to trust that things will work out as we want. And when they do, we are happy, and when they don't, we have to explain to ourselves why God did not favor our request. But here, we are being asked to trust in God even when things go directly against our will.

Although this seems to be a much more challenging level of trust, in fact, it reflects something that most people will already have experienced in their own lives: what appears at first to be a great blessing turns out to be a disaster, and what is initially perceived as a loss, in time comes to be seen as a gift.

I learned that lesson from my own experience with the collapse of my business. When that happened, I went to a very dark place. But, ultimately, that disaster led me to my encounter with the Mussar tradition and put me on a path to a more fulfilling life than I could have hoped for as a film producer.

The classic case of this sort of reversal is the well-documented impact on people's lives when they win a lot of money in a lottery. In 2016, when the main prize in the PowerBall lottery stood at $1.5 billion, *Time* magazine published an article entitled, "Here's How Winning the Lottery Makes You Miserable,"[14] which included capsule life stories of people who won huge amounts of money. Most echoed the view of Jack Whittaker, who won $315 million in a lottery, who is quoted in the story saying, "I wish that we had torn the ticket up." There may have been elation at the moment, but that good fortune too often ended in bankruptcy, divorce, loneliness, drugs, and suicide.

Practicing *bitachon* like this means seeing the hand of God in everything that happens and then stepping away from the very human tendency to sort our experiences into the categories of good and bad events. Instead, one trusts that *everything* that God does, God does for the best because God is inherently good and always wants the best for us, even if we can't see it at the moment.

That attitude is palatable when things turn out as they did for Rabbi Akiva in the field and me in the ending of my business but becomes much more inaccessible when we focus on some things that happen to people in their lives where it seems impossible to perceive any good—like murder, rape, innocent people caught up in the ravages of war, and that glaring example in our time, the Holocaust, as well as any other genocide.

Rabbi Akiva's worldview was not restricted to what happens in this life, and he included the afterlife in his calculus. This became a central tenet of Judaism, which is that rewards earned in this life may come to be paid in the World-to-Come. There is no guarantee of reward in this world or this lifetime, says Rabbeinu Yonah,[15] because "we know that this reward is guaranteed only in the World-to-Come."[16]

Taking that extended view of life makes Rabbi Akiva's position more understandable, though our ability to trust may still be challenged when we are in the throes of our own difficulties in human life.

Refraction #4: Destiny Is Malleable

There is another way of practicing *bitachon* with such complete, intense, total trust that it actually alters the reality in which I live. This level of *bitachon* is so powerful that it can change what was destined to happen.

Rabbi Yitzchak Volozhiner, who succeeded his father as head of the premier European yeshiva in 1821, wrote: "One who has *bitachon* with his whole heart is not afraid of bad tidings, and has no worries, and the *bitachon* itself is the reason he is saved from misfortune."[17]

In this view, *bitachon* is not just an attitude; it is an active force that has an impact on what actually takes place in one's life. Because *bitachon* can have an impact on reality, this brings into focus the question of how much effort a person ought to expend in trying to bring a situation to a desired conclusion. Is a person entitled to put all their trust in God and therefore not lift a finger on their own behalf? Or are we obligated to take some action to sort out our problems using the natural means that are available to us? And, if the latter, how much effort is warranted?

This is a hotly debated subject going right back to the Talmud,[18] where we find an argument between Rabbi Yishmael, who asserts that a person must always make efforts within the ways of the world, and Rabbi Shimon bar Yochai, who takes the position that intense dedication to Torah study obviates the need for any effort whatsoever.

The Talmud concludes that "Multitudes did as Rabbi Yishmael and were successful, while others did as Rabbi Shimon bar Yochai and were not successful."

That answer seems conclusive until we look at it more closely and realize that the fact that "multitudes" were not successful in Rabbi Shimon's approach does not exclude the possibility that "individuals" were, indeed, successful through his way. If we assume that the more a person perfects trust in God, the less human action is necessary to bring about the desired results, then that opens the way for certain individuals to have perfected their trust to such a degree that they need to make no effort whatsoever to solve their problems. In fact, making an effort would be a demonstration of lack of trust and would therefore weaken the impact of their trust.

This was the position of the Alter of Novardok. When he was asked about the statement that many attempted to follow Rabbi Shimon bar

Yochai's way and failed, the Alter pointed to the key word "multitude."[19] Rabbi Shimon's way was surely not for the masses. But individuals can strive to reach this powerful manifestation of trust and succeed.

This conviction was converted into practice. The very elite among Novardok students in nineteenth-century eastern Europe would set out on foot to strange communities without a penny in their pockets. As they moved about, they would abstain from speech, not asking for a ride or even for food. Upon reaching a town, they would enter the local study hall and, without a word to anyone, sit and learn. They relied totally on God for their needs, without the least direct effort on their part to provide for themselves. And, in general, their trust was rewarded, and food arrived!

What's at work here is the conviction that cultivating complete, deep trust in God can be so powerful as to transform a person fundamentally. And when we make that kind of profound change in ourselves, we make ourselves worthy of a new reality. This notion holds that God can tolerate several alternative realities simultaneously, in potential, and it is only our action of becoming worthy that determines which reality becomes manifest in this world. Our worthiness is determined by our *bitachon*.

Seventh Day Trust

Observance of Shabbat, as well as experiencing its impact, is built on a foundation of trust. When we look at what the Torah says about the very first Shabbat the slaves, newly freed from Egypt, were to observe in the wilderness, we see that it is framed as a test of trust. God promises to feed the people with food that daily falls from the sky, and then Moses cautions them about Shabbat, saying that the *manna* will not fall that day. Nevertheless:

some of the people went out on the seventh day to gather, but they found nothing. And God said to Moses, "How long will you people refuse to obey My commandments and My teachings? Mark that the Lord has given you Shabbat; therefore, God gives you two days' food on the sixth day. Let everyone remain where he is; let no one leave his place on the seventh day."[20]

As we saw in Chapter 3, the *manna* is often depicted in the Mussar literature as a test of trust because that God-given food could only be collected daily. If kept overnight, it rotted. Every day, the people had to put their trust in God that they would be fed. But on Friday, they needed to trust even more because they were promised that they would be given an additional portion in order to be freed from the labor of collecting on the seventh day itself.

Our situation is parallel. Observing Shabbat means setting aside all productive and constructive activities that support our lives on the material plane in order to experience a true day of rest. That act of setting aside requires trust, or you simply won't be able to do it.

Isaiah (30:15) draws the connection between the other sorts of qualities we have been looking at and trust:

> For this is what the Lord God, Holy One of Israel, has said: "In sitting still and pleasant rest you will be saved, in quietness and trust shall be your strength."

The prophet adds trust to the list of key traits that characterize Shabbat.

The great sage of the eighteenth century, the Vilna Gaon,[21] connects trust to another of the traits we have delved into, which is *histapkut*, meaning "sufficiency." He wrote:

> Trust and enoughness are general principles for all good character traits. And they are the opposite of desire and greed.

On Shabbat, we say to ourselves that we have made our best efforts six days of the week, and now we take on the attitude that all our needs have been met with no further effort required.

But the Vilna Gaon concludes: "And the central factor of everything is trust."

The Israelites faced a test of trust in the desert. But when we look at the test we face on Shabbat, ours is actually greater. Why? Because when they went out to gather on Shabbat, they found that there was nothing to be had. We, on the other hand, can easily keep working, keep sending emails, go to the bank, go shopping to catch that item before it is sold out, or before the sale ends, because in the society in which we live, Saturday is just another day. It takes a deliberately and purposefully chosen act of trust for us to be able to lay it all down.

And more subtly, even if you have put away the car keys and turned off the computer, it takes a strong sense of trust to allow yourself to enter into the inner states of sufficiency, rest, harmony, stillness, and joy that we have been exploring, rather than slipping into worrying and fretting about all the things that need doing and that you are neglecting that day. Trust is the antidote to worry.

The key element in trust is the recognition that what is happening is not all about me. I am a very small part of something vastly vaster; I am not the ruler of the world, not even the ruler of my small part of it. Six days a week, we act as though we are the central actors in our lives, and then, when we separate from mundane life on Shabbat, we encounter the more profound reality that, in truth, we are masters of very little in our lives. We set down our life-building activities, calling on the same trust that the Israelites exhibited in the desert, trusting that heaven will deliver a double portion for us on Friday so that we can enter the realm of holiness on the seventh day.

Shabbat can be a great teacher about rest, quiet, joy, peace, and the other traits we have been looking at, but foremost among them is the inner sensibility that there is a much greater force in our lives on whom we can and do rely. What makes it possible to loosen our grip on the steering wheel of our lives on Shabbat is dipping into a reservoir of trust that it is okay to relinquish the effort to control our lives. But still greater is the revelation it delivers that the control we strive to exercise over our lives is actually an illusion in the first place. Shabbat practice teaches us that the locus of control in our lives is not in our own hands. True, we are not powerless, but neither are we anywhere near as powerful as we seem to believe we are responsible to be. This insight is something that can then accompany us even as we are active in productive activities during the other six days of the week. This is true for the individual, the family, the community, the city, the nation-state, and beyond.

And so, to recap, laying down our projects and our responsibilities for Shabbat is an act of trust. We've looked at four different refractions of what it can mean to trust in God:

1. Resignation—since I am not going to engage with any mundane matters, I might as well just relax and enjoy Shabbat.

2. God will take care of it. God is looking out for me, and I trust that what I hope for will happen.

3. God is good, and whatever God causes to happen, even if it looks bad to me right now, I trust it is for the good.

4. Trust changes reality. When trust is total, that powerful force transforms me, and once I am different, I am entitled to a different reality. Trust changes destiny.

Developing Trust

One of the best techniques to grow in trusting God is to memorize certain phrases and repeat them over and over like a mantra.

One such phrase that fits our current focus comes from the prayer said at the end of Shabbat, in the Havdalah ceremony:

Evtach v'lo efchad—"I will trust and will not fear."

Another phrase that might be meaningful to you is:

God knows what is best for me.

Or you can adopt or even create another phrase, as long as it holds the meaning you relate to under the heading of trust.

By repeating these phrases again and again, they start to sink in. You begin to recognize on an *emotional and intuitive level* that "I don't really know anything with certainty."

In time, you will become better at doing what we human beings find so difficult to do—to accept what has been decreed for us with trust and even joy.

8

Holiness

The Holy

In two short words, the Torah assigns us our mission in life: *kedoshim tihiyu*, it says. "You shall be holy."[1] There is no directive to be tall or wealthy or popular or successful. Our mission is higher than any of those things because the essence of a human being is spiritual, and in telling us to pursue holiness, the Torah is directing us to reach for our highest human spiritual potential. And since this injunction is stated in the plural, we can take it that it applies to every single one of us, including you and me.

But what is holiness and how do we acquire it? One thing is certain: it cannot be defined. The biblical verse that gives us the injunction to pursue holiness—"You shall be holy"—offers a sort of explanation by saying, "because I, the Lord your God, am holy." What we learn from this is that, by its nature, holiness is a thoroughly spiritual quality that is closely associated with the divine. There is no way the small boxes of language could possibly contain and define something so vast and sublime.

When his personal secretary and editor, Rabbi David Cohen, asked the poet and mystic, Rabbi Avraham Isaac Kook (1865–1935), the first Ashkenazi Chief Rabbi of Israel, for a definition of the holy, the answer he received was, "Holiness is the quality that is revealed in the holy."[2]

Rabbi Cohen himself concludes: "The nature of the holy itself is without a definition because it is the deepest of the deep, the beginning of everything, and it is not given to be explained in a definition."

Still, the medieval commentator Rashi had to say something to explain to us what it means to be holy, and he interpreted it to mean, "you shall be separate." Holiness refers to something or someone that has been "set apart," and what differentiates this separateness from, say, quarantine or solitary confinement is that what has been set apart in the case of holiness is being reserved for a special purpose related to God, the ultimate in the Holy.

That doesn't exactly tell us what holiness is in itself, but it does start to help us make sense of what is involved with the holy. The notion of "set apart for a special purpose related to God" applies broadly to all the holy days on the Jewish calendar, as well as to holy places and people. The word for holiness in Hebrew is *kedusha,* and all these times, places, and objects are designated by some variant of that word.

For example, we find that the Torah proclaimed[3] certain days to be "times of holy assembly." These *mikrei kodesh* are set apart from the other days of the year and include the holy festivals of Shavuot, Yom Kippur, Sukkot, and the like.

Similarly, certain places are identified as holy, prime examples being the land of Israel—the Holy Land—and also Jerusalem, the Holy City, and within Jerusalem, the Holy Temple. These places are each unique in their category, bounded off, and dedicated to God.

The same notion can apply to property or even money that became consecrated when someone dedicated a gift to the needs of the Temple in Jerusalem. An owner would declare an object or animal to be *hekdesh*—consecrated—and it was then set aside to be offered to God in holy service.

There are, of course, holy people. The biblical high priest was commanded to wear a banner on his forehead that declared, "Holy to God,"[4] and given his unique and special role in society, that designation fits within the territory of "set apart for a special purpose related to God."

The same holds true for Shabbat *kodesh*—the holy Sabbath—which is actually listed among the "times of holy assembly" mentioned above. Shabbat is a day set aside to be infused with divine presence, separate from the mundane quality of the other six days of the week.

The Holiness of the Day

Unlike us, Shabbat does not have to "become" holy, because the Torah tells us explicitly[5] that Shabbat was made holy from the moment that it was originally created:

On the seventh day God had finished the work God had been doing; so on that day God rested from all God's work. Then God blessed the seventh day and made it holy.

When we apply Rashi's understanding of holiness to Shabbat, it is so obvious that Shabbat is meant to be separate and set apart from the other six days of the week. It is marked and bounded as a unique day, completely unlike any other day of the week. The Torah[6] makes that point directly:

Six days you shall labor, but on the seventh day you shall rest; even during the plowing season and harvest you must rest.

Six days are for work and the seventh is set aside and dedicated to the divine quality of holiness. Because God made Shabbat holy, we can conclude that the holiness of Shabbat is an inherent, independent and enduring quality that is part of the fundamental nature of the day itself, from the moment of its creation.

But if that were to be the whole story, wouldn't we be just passengers on a train that passes through the holy station of Shabbat, with no role to play in that holiness? That can't be, because in the fourth of the Ten Commandments we are told explicitly, "Remember the day of Shabbat to sanctify it." We are assigned an active role in sanctifying the seventh day.

This idea fits with the thinking of Rabbi Meir Simcha of Dvinsk, known as the *Meshech Chochma* (1843–1926), who took the view that nothing is inherently holy. In his perspective, human beings have a crucial role in the process of sanctification. He wrote:

> Do not imagine that the Temple and Tabernacle are intrinsically holy. Far be it! The Almighty dwells amidst God's children and if they transgress the covenant, these structures become divested of all their holiness. . . . Even the Tablets—"the writing of God"—were not intrinsically holy, but only so on account of you. . . . To sum up, there is nothing intrinsically holy in the world except the Lord, to whom alone reverence, praise and homage is due.

We find ourselves facing an apparent contradiction. On the one hand, we are told that on the seventh day, God not only created Shabbat but also sanctified it. And on the other, it is apparently given over to human beings to be the agents of the sanctification of this special day.

The resolution is found right in the central prayers for Shabbat morning, the Amidah, in which the thirteen blessings that make up the core section of the weekday prayer are replaced with one special blessing relating to the sanctity of Shabbat. The blessing concludes: "Blessed are You, O God, Who sanctifies the Sabbath."

Through these words, we invoke and acknowledge the primal sanctification wrought by the One Above, but it is *we* who are making these statements and, in so doing, we participate in sanctifying the day. Far from being contradictory, one reinforces the other. Our words acknowledge the holiness of Shabbat, and in uttering those words, we are directing our bodies and minds toward the dimension of the holy and the One who created it.

From this perspective, Shabbat is not holy just because that quality is written into its DNA. Even if that is true, it still falls to us to act in ways that lift up and make manifest that sanctity and, conversely, not to act in ways that diminish or demolish it in any way.

The rabbis in the Talmud are clear in acknowledging that we have a role to play in bringing sanctity to Shabbat, but when they ask how we are supposed to do that, their answer is surprising: "Remember it over wine,"[7] they said.

This is the source for the ritual of reciting a blessing over a cup of wine on Shabbat—*kiddush*, a word that comes from the same linguistic root as all references to holiness in Hebrew. When we make a Shabbat blessing over wine, we are fulfilling the Torah's directive to remember and proclaim the holiness of Shabbat, as the verse commands.

But why wine? Perhaps what the rabbis had in mind was that we enjoy a drink just so we enter Shabbat in a jolly mood, as the Psalm says: "Wine gladdens a person's heart."[8] But that's too simple. And, in fact, the prophet Hosea even cautions that "wine leads the heart astray."[9] What else might be at work here?

When, on Friday evening, we raise the cup of wine and make the accompanying verbal declaration, we set a boundary, in word and deed, proclaiming that we are now making the crossing over into sacred time. Lifting the cup and speaking our words calls attention to the line over which we are about to step, on the other side of which lies holiness. Shabbat is a time set apart that is meant to be qualitatively different from the other six days. The seventh day is separated off for the special purpose of bringing us into communion with the holy and with the Holy One.

Wine is a brilliantly appropriate agent for consecrating Shabbat, not because of the effects of alcohol, but because in wine we find a metaphor for the transformation of the mundane into the sacred that applies equally to Shabbat as well as to ourselves.

Wine starts out as ordinary grapes. The fermentation process turns the fruit juice into a quite different product. Grape juice is basically fruit-flavored water that costs pennies, whereas wine is a complex, subtle, and nuanced liquid that costs many dollars.

Grape juice represents the natural world and wine the spiritual dimension that is the inherent potential within it. Wine actually defies nature because, in nature, as time passes, most things degrade, whereas wine, as it ages, improves and becomes more precious.

We can see that in wine we find an archetype of the natural rendered spiritual. And in just the same way, Shabbat is a slice of ordinary time transformed into the sacred. This view of *kiddush* fulfills the intention Rabbi Abraham Joshua Heschel attributed to Shabbat ritual:

> The law of the Sabbath tries to direct the body and the mind to the dimension of the holy. It tries to teach us that [humanity] stands not only in a relation to nature but in a relation also to the Creator of nature.

And, indeed, the text of the blessing for *kiddush* is focused not on the wine itself but on "the Creator of the fruit of the vine."

Grape juice, put through a process of refinement, becomes wine. The same applies to us. We, too, start out as unrefined raw material. As we age, we learn and grow, but the Torah directs us to aim still higher than that. It advises us to aspire to lift up the physical and mundane to enter into the spiritual and holy. We embody this deep symbolism when we raise the cup of wine and step over the line from ordinary time into the holiness of Shabbat.

This is meaningful symbolism, but it does not exhaust what the ritual of *kiddush* has to teach us. There is another lesson in the fact that the verbal formula for *kiddush* is directed to the wine, which is the agent of sanctification. The wine is the focus of the blessing, yet the fact remains that we do not make *kiddush* without a cup. We pour the wine into the cup, lift the two together, and then recite the blessing.

This, too, is symbolic, though in this case the focus is not on what is said or done but on the person who is performing the ritual. The cup represents the religious form, which is solid, and the wine represents the spiritual essence, which is fluid. Both are integral components of the whole ritual. Although the priority clearly falls on the side of the spiritual since the blessing focuses on the wine and the cup is not even mentioned, nevertheless, except in the most extreme situations,[10] both are necessary.

In our observance of Shabbat, the focus should be on the spiritual, but we need to acknowledge and accept the crucial role played by the "cup" of structure because, without a cup, the wine dribbles away.

Creating Holiness

Establishing these ideas sets up our exploration of how holiness can take a place in our own practice of Shabbat, and the transformative impact that practice can have on our lives.

We have already seen that the notions of holiness and sanctification are built into the rituals of Shabbat. But we have to note that the Torah not only charges us to sanctify Shabbat, but it also gives us the directive to sanctify ourselves. When the Torah states, "You shall be holy," it is actually laying before us the Jewish statement of the highest purpose and goal that exists for a human life, and that is to be holy.

We are charged to sanctify Shabbat and to sanctify ourselves, and the key question I want to bring into focus now is how can we engage with Shabbat in such a way as to foster that holiness in ourselves?

In one way, this is a difficult question to answer. After many years of studying every text I could find that deals with holiness from a Jewish perspective, I have reached the conclusion that holiness is elusive, and our rabbis give us very few things we can do to address sanctification directly. There is no recipe or formula that guarantees that, as long as you do A + B + C, you will generate holiness. What our teachers emphasize instead is that there are things we can do that can clear the way for holiness to come to us, if that be the will of heaven.

Rabbi Moshe Chaim Luzzatto, toward the end of his eighteenth-century book, *Path of the Just*, has a chapter on holiness in which he says:

> The matter of holiness is dual. Its beginning is work while its end is reward; its beginning is exertion while its end is a gift. That is, its beginning is that which a person does to sanctify oneself, while its end is one's being sanctified. This is what our sages, of blessed memory, said: "If a person sanctifies himself a little, he becomes much sanctified. If he sanctifies himself below, he becomes sanctified from above." (Yoma 39a)

Refocusing back on our topic of Shabbat, we can wonder what efforts we can make regarding Shabbat that will open the way to receiving the gift of holiness?

One of the primary practices that shows up in almost every form of observance on Shabbat has to do with marking and respecting boundaries. The holy time of Shabbat begins sharply at a certain moment and ends at a certain moment. Some activities, like writing or using a computer, get parked at the line we draw to mark off Shabbat and are only resumed once the holy day is declared over. Shopping and the use of money are proscribed. In these and many other examples, what we see at play is the principle that what has the potential to be holy will only be holy as long as we separate it from the mundane.

That principle applies to us as well. We prepare ourselves to receive the gift of holiness by taking steps to set ourselves apart and distinct from the ordinary activities and concerns of our worldly lives.

A paradigm for this principle shows up in the incident in the Bible when Moses catches sight of the burning bush and goes over to have a look at this strange phenomenon. God says, "Do not come any closer. Take off your sandals, for the place where you are standing is holy ground."[11]

Now, in all likelihood, that particular piece of mountainside did not look a whole lot different from every other patch of Middle Eastern dirt and shrubs that surrounded it. But, in fact, it was totally different—"the place where you are standing is holy ground"—and that difference needed a marker to highlight its holiness. In this case, that marker was created by removing shoes.

Similarly for us, when we perform the actions that serve to separate Shabbat from the other six days of the week, we mark it as having a special purpose relating to the presence of the divine in the world.

By setting and observing boundaries that signify the special quality of Shabbat, we sanctify the day and, in the process, prepare ourselves for our own sanctification. Put simply, by doing things that set boundaries to mark off sacred time, place, and activities, we open a space that is prepared to be inhabited by the divine presence, both in the realm of Shabbat and within our own inner lives.

There are other sorts of boundaries we can establish for Shabbat that also prepare the way for holiness. In fact, that idea can be employed as a test we can apply to anything we might say or do on Shabbat. We can ask ourselves, "Is what I am about to do or say in the spirit of holiness?" and then we can choose to do only those things where we can answer in the affirmative.

We discussed in a previous chapter the prohibition on getting angry on Shabbat, and it isn't hard to see that speaking harshly to someone else, or even getting inflamed with anger ourselves, are not the sorts of things that would pass the "holiness test." For the same reason, gossiping, spreading rumors, telling lies, arguing, and the like also fail that test, whereas words of kindness, joy, love, and compassion would fall on the other side of the line. If we think of holiness as the most refined, ephemeral, exalted spiritual level to which we can aspire, far beyond the egocentric thoughts and activities that usually fill our days, it becomes clear why included among the traditional laws of Shabbat is the prohibition on speaking about anything that might distress or pain another person. That, too, is not consonant with the holy nature of the day, and being the one who spreads the gossip or delivers the distressing news is not consistent with our own ascent to holiness.

This idea is alluded to in Psalm 24, where the question is asked, "Who may ascend the mountain of God, and who can stand in God's holy place?"

The answer: "One with clean hands and pure heart."

In other words, if we want to qualify ourselves to be receptacles of holiness, we have to avoid words and deeds that in any way sully the hands and heart. There are tomes that tell us what to watch out for, and there is the compass of conscience as well.[12]

By marking out Shabbat as a day that is separated for the purposes of holiness, and then actively sanctifying it through our words and actions, we fulfill the religious nature of the seventh day. At the same time, if we consciously enter into this process of sanctification, the actions we take have an impact on ourselves as actors, making us more fitting to be holy, and thus advancing us toward completing our spiritual nature.

The goal of holiness is so thoroughly spiritual and so elevated that it only has relevance to our lives if we take the radical step of willingly forgoing and separating ourselves from the mundane. That is exactly what happens on Shabbat, when we elevate our lives spiritually by disconnecting from the secular. We, who are created in the divine image, have the capacity to draw holiness into the world in time and place, as well as into ourselves, when we create a separation from the ordinary and then invite more of the Divine Presence to rest in that place, time, object, or person.

These ideas are stated clearly by Rabbi Eliyahu Dessler, a prominent product of the Kelm Mussar yeshiva who died in 1954. Rav Dessler writes:[13]

> We call Shabbat "the Holy Sabbath." Holiness means to be ready for the highest endeavors, to aim for the noblest goals. The essence of Shabbat is to free oneself from the negative, narrow values of materialism and to adopt the boundless values of the spirit. The prohibitions against certain labors in all their ramifications are based on this principle. [Their purpose is to divert our creativity from the physical sphere to the realm of the spirit.]

Our aim to experience and internalize the holy on Shabbat provides us with both a goal and a practice. Shabbat is a day on which to engage more fully than at any other time in living in a way that is entirely spiritual. Indeed, we can take that as another refraction of the meaning of holiness: living in a way that is entirely spiritual.

As God is completely spiritual with no trace of a material existence, so should you, too, strive to be completely spiritual with no trace of a material existence. That's not really possible for us, of course, but at least for one day a week, we can lift ourselves as high as we are humanly able. On Shabbat, we strive to live life from within our soul dimension. With this idea in mind, we can better understand some of the traditional practices that are legislated for Shabbat.

For example, shopping is not a Shabbat activity. At first glance, this seems like just a restriction, a prohibition. But from the perspective of living life from your soul dimension, this constraint becomes obvious. Your soul has no pockets in which to carry a wallet. And whatever you might buy is very unlikely to be intended for the soul.

That logic applies to many other activities that are proscribed for Shabbat. Would you want to be a passenger in a car being driven by your soul? Would you want your soul to write your emails? Do your cooking? Mail your packages?

More to the point, would your soul want to do these sorts of mundane activities? Not if the goal were holiness.

We need to underline that giving up the material and the secular on Shabbat for the sake of the holy and the spiritual is not a call to be ascetic. The Sages of the Talmud tell us that "[Shabbat] was given only for eating and drinking."[14] In practice, eating fine food and drinking delicious beverages is entirely consistent with the goals of the day, because elevating the physical to a higher, sublime level is consonant with the quest to bring holiness into our life. That consistency is reinforced when we recall the teaching of the Alter of Slabodka we encountered in the chapter on joy, who advocated for enjoying physical pleasure on Shabbat, and his thinking extends so far as to link that sort of pleasure with holiness. Hear his words:[15]

> We find that the holiness of Shabbat also extends to physical pleasures, to the point that they also become holy, and it is impossible to sanctify Shabbat except through them. We find that in the entire creation, that its holiness is not expressed except through physical pleasures.

This principle gives meaning to so much of what we do on Shabbat. In order to create the space for holiness, we mark out clear boundaries that serve to keep out the mundane. And that bounded space we create is now open to be filled with undistracted prayer, communing with God and other people, and enjoying the pleasures of the day through good food and drink. When we mark Shabbat by dressing in finery, setting a beautiful table, and investing in fine candlesticks and a *kiddush* cup, that, too, can be spiritual practice, because beauty is itself a spiritual quality.

In this way, Shabbat becomes a day set apart for spiritual matters and spiritual pleasures, but a word of caution is in order. We also need to remember the words of Ramban (Nachmanides), who tells us that holiness is not just a matter of avoiding things that defile us; we also need to be self-restrained in doing things that are permitted to us. Otherwise, we risk becoming what he calls "a vile person with the permission of the Torah."

Pleasure on Shabbat is not meant to be sensory indulgence, but a practice that lifts the physical side of our existence up to the realm of the spiritual. As Rabbi Eliyahu Dessler puts it:[16]

> The holiness of Shabbat is so great that it can absorb these physical pleasures and others too, into the sphere of spirituality. It is the transformation of bodily activities into the sphere of holiness which is the hallmark of the World to Come.

And recall that Shabbat is considered to be a taste in this life of the glory of the World to Come.

We have made good use of Rashi's view that holiness is a quality that can infuse any vessel that is set aside and consecrated for a purpose related to God, but there is another important aspect to holiness, and that is our own experience of the holy. Rabbi Perr once said to me about holiness that it was an experience of cleansing that he had felt as a result of being in the presence of holy people. There is a sublime delight in being alive in moments when the air (and your heart) glows with the light of holiness, and it is in your hand to create the space within which that can happen, beginning by carving out a time when you set aside email, politics, conflict, material desires, and the myriad mundane activities that seem to have a lien on our every moment.

Within that bounded space that keeps at bay all the preoccupations of the other six days of the week, you have the possibility of coming to complete stillness. The primary meaning of the word *shabbat* is "to cease," and in those moments when you come to a full stop, you make it possible for holiness to catch up with you. Then you can bask, motionless, in its glory.

Rav Kook writes:[17]

The highest holiness is the holiness of stillness, the holiness of existence, when a person recognizes oneself as nullified in their private internal being, and lives a universal life, the life of all . . . and one elevates all of existence with him to its Source.

Becoming Holy

What draws you into the material side of existence and away from the spiritual? Is it how much time you spend involved with material things, like clothes, or a car, or domestic gadgets or objects? Or even a tendency to steer all conversations toward politics? What might it be for you?

Once you have identified one or more of those areas of your life where you can see that you are prone to being immersed in the material and the mundane, make it a practice for a number of Shabbats to separate yourself from one or two of those activities for this one day of the week, for the sake of experiencing the spiritual and the holy. In this way, you will taste for yourself what it is like to leave off the mundane for the sake of the sacred.

Once you review and decide on the activities that meet the criteria and that you pledge to set aside for Shabbat, write them down. If you have the practice of journaling, you can write them in your journal. Or (or, additionally), you can write them on a piece of paper or a post-it note to be seen on Shabbat as a reminder to yourself.

And in time, you can extend that practice to more Shabbats or indefinitely.

We also touched on the idea of applying a mental test before you do or say anything on Shabbat, which is to ask yourself: "Is what I am about to do or say in the spirit of holiness?" Keep that question at the ready in your mind to interrogate anything you might be about to say or do, and observe what effect it has in determining what you then go on to do or say.

To guide your journaling, you can ask yourself questions like:

- What sorts of things exert the pull of material existence to draw me away from the spiritual on Shabbat?

- What could—or did—I do to overcome that pull toward the material?

- What boundaries did I draw? And how did I do in respecting those boundaries?

- Did those choices and actions have any impact on the feeling of spirituality I experienced on Shabbat?

- Did you make a practice of asking yourself the question—"Is what I am about to do or say in the spirit of holiness?" What effect could you detect that question having on your speech and actions?

Conclusion

Sources suggest and personal experience confirms that the practice of a weekly day of rest can be so much more than just a much-needed recharge. As you take on certain activities and avoid others, you deliver to yourself a curated set of experiences that, over time, leave their impression and ingrain a new inner reality in you. That transformation shows up not just on Shabbat, but on all the other six days of the week as well. When embraced with this intention, the Shabbat effect leads you to become more the person you have the potential to be and, I have good reason to speculate, you actually already want to be.

We have focused on how following the traditions of a day of rest contributes to developing more awareness, contentment, joy, peace, rest, trust, and more. But you should not just take my word for it. What you learn from your own experience is infinitely more valuable than things you hear from another person, book, or course. The benefits of practicing Shabbat will become vividly clear to your mind only when you engage actively in the sorts of things we have been talking about here.

You can and should look forward to experiencing rest, joy, and awareness on your Shabbat, but at the same time, it is entirely predictable that as you seek out peace, joy, and delight, you will encounter resistance and irritation as well. Any effort to grow spiritually tends to trigger inner challenges that need to be worked through for that growth to take place.

You want to be punctual, but others are slower, and you get annoyed. You want to enjoy the delight of a beautiful dinner, but the potatoes are not only burnt but also cold. Where's the pleasure? The people around the table are boring—and seem especially so when you think about all the events on Friday evening that you are missing out on.

This phenomenon is not only well-documented in Jewish sources, but it is given a name, which in Hebrew is *yetzer ha'ra*. The term translates literally as the "evil inclination" and is often described as "the inner adversary." You set out to do something with the goal of elevating yourself, and in the private theater of your own mind, a drama ensues in which temptation, self-criticism, laziness, rationalization, and despair all have their parts to play in undermining your efforts and holding you back from achieving the goal you have set for yourself to pursue.

In wondrous reflection of the uniqueness of every human being, the script followed by the *yetzer ha'ra* is entirely personalized.

Not everyone is prone to laziness, but if you are, then your inner adversary will whisper, "Why bother?"

If you are anxious about what other people think, you may hear a voice saying, "You don't want to turn on your phone, but a little peek can't hurt."

The morose person is liable to have thoughts about how impossible it is to delight and be joyful, so why even try?

And so it goes, according to the personal proclivities and vulnerabilities of your own inner life. You can and should expect that every effort you make to lift yourself up toward becoming more whole and more holy will encounter a force of gravity that tries to pull you down. And so the journey of ascent involves not only making plans for all the good things you will engage in but also having a clear expectation that you will face challenges that you will need to overcome.

The *yetzer ha'ra* that I am talking about here is called the "evil inclination" and, at first glance, it appears to be an entirely negative force, but it's not so. Your efforts to defy that inner force of gravity have the effect of building up the strength you need to achieve and then sustain the growth you seek. Change requires new muscles, and persisting in pursuing your ideals in the face of resistance is exactly how you develop that inner capacity. From this perspective, the inner adversary is not evil: it is a tough but friendly personal trainer.

When you make an effort to do something differently and it goes so smoothly, just as much as when you try to take on a new behavior and find yourself bombarded by undermining thoughts, it is certain that your experiences contain valuable lessons for you. Mussar students not only study the teachings handed down to us by wise ancestors from previous generations, but we also pay very close attention to the lessons that can be uncovered in our own experiences. Being aware of your own tendencies, and especially the areas in your inner life where challenges tend to show up—often in the voice of the *yetzer ha'ra*—offers you unparalleled guidance on the path that leads to your future.

Just as the inner adversary has its own name, so does the practice of learning from your own experience, including your predictable encounters with your *yetzer ha'ra*. This process is called *hitlamdut*, a term that literally means "teaching yourself." It is well outlined by the quite recent Mussar teacher, Rabbi Shlomo Wolbe,[1] whose words describe well how profoundly important it is to be a student of your own experiences, so you can learn from them and not lose out on the lessons they contain:[2]

Anyone who wants to "work on themself" must understand well the depth of this matter and must agree and commit to the fundamental practice of *hitlamdut* from now and throughout one's life, in all one's affairs being only a learner, until the day of death. Even when one reaches the time of death, one should not be dying, but rather learning how to die. This is the way of the practitioner of Mussar.

When you take on the practice of observing Shabbat—whether it is something new for you or you are seeking to find a more spiritual and growth-oriented way to engage in its observance—and you scrutinize the experiences that get sparked in you, you are sure to be able to extract valuable lessons that are applicable just to you. You'll see your strengths, and you will also get just as clear a picture of what in you still has more potential to be strengthened. Digging out and acting on those lessons is how I developed my own Shabbat practice and saw its impact throughout my life, and I encourage you to try, learn, and grow. *Hitlamdut*—teaching yourself from your own experiences—is the single most important thing you can take on as you walk the path to becoming a more whole and holy person—on Shabbat and the other six days of the week as well.

Let's close with the final words of the Psalm for Shabbat[3] that is traditionally recited three times in the traditional synagogue liturgy. It reads:

> The righteous shall flourish like the palm-tree; They will grow like a cedar in Lebanon.
> Planted in the house of God,
> They shall flourish in the courts of our God.
> They shall still bring forth fruit in old age; They shall be fresh and flourishing;
> attesting that God is upright, my Rock, in whom there is no wrong.

My wish is that this be true for you: May your practice of a day of rest help you flourish like a palm tree, which produces sweet and nourishing fruit. And may you grow tall and mighty like a cedar, the ideal wood for building strong and lasting structures. May your life be fresh, and may you thrive in it.

And may we meet again soon, to be good companions on this ascending path of life we are walking together, directing our footsteps toward becoming more whole and more holy people.

Glossary

he'elam: a lapse in awareness that leads to inadvertent transgression, from the linguistic root that means "to disappear" or "to vanish."

hekdesh: consecrated

histapkut: sufficiency; simplicity; enoughness

hitlamdut: teaching yourself from your own experiences

kiddush: ritual recitation of a blessing over a cup of wine

kodesh: holy

kotzer: harvesting

menucha: rest

middot: lit. measures; traits of character

nefesh: the dimension of the soul most closely associated with the body and the emotions

neshama: the most spiritual dimension of the soul, said to be hewn from God's Throne of Glory

seder: order

Shabbat: the Hebrew term for the seventh day of the week from which the English word "Sabbath" derives, from the linguistic root that can mean "cease" or "sit" or "return."

shalom: peace; harmony

ta'anit dibbur: a "fast" of silence

tzom shtikah: a "fast" from speech

yetzer ha'ra: the so-called evil inclination that presents challenges to our efforts to elevate ourselves

zehirut: caution; watchfulness; bright awareness

Notes

A Note on Practice

1 For more on the full range of Mussar practices, see my *Everyday Holiness*, Part III.

Introduction

1 When the book *Duties of the Heart*, by Rabbi Bahya ibn Paquda, was published.

2 In his *Sichos Mussar*, 12–13.

3 *Da'at, Chachmah uMussar*, 112.

4 *Happiness and the Human Spirit* (Woodstock, VT: Jewish Lights, 2007).

5 *Sha'arei Kedushah* [Gates of Holiness], Part 1, Gate 2.

6 The Jewish tradition that the Torah contains 613 commandments was first recorded in the third century CE when it was mentioned in the Talmud (Makkot 23b).

7 Genesis Rabbah 44:1; a commentary on the book of Genesis, probably written between 300 and 500 CE, with some later additions.

8 Refined: *tziruf*; jeweler: *tzoref*.

9 Exodus 20:9–11.

10 The Hebrew term from which the English word "Sabbath" derives.

11 Leviticus 19:2.

12 The literature comparing and contrasting and sometimes trying to reconcile religion and spirituality is voluminous. See, for example, Schneiders, Sandra Marie. "Religion and Spirituality: Strangers, Rivals, or Partners?" *The Santa Clara Lectures* 6, no. 2 (February 6, 2000).

13 Rabbi Shlomo ben Yitzchak, 1040–105, Troyes, France, known by the acronym "*Rashi*," was a medieval French rabbi, the author of comprehensive commentaries on the Talmud and Hebrew Bible.

14 Exodus 31:15.

15 *Sichot Mussar*, Part I, Mir Yeshiva, 1979, 40.

16 For example: *Sabbath: Finding Rest, Renewal, and Delight in Our Busy Lives* by Wayne Muller; *Sabbath Keeping: Finding Freedom in the Rhythms of Rest* by Lynne M. Baab; *The Rest of God: Restoring Your Soul by Restoring Sabbath* by Mark Buchanan, *24/6: The Power of Unplugging One Day a Week* by Tiffany Shlain, among many others.

17 J. A. Olson, D. A. Sandra, S. P. L. Veissière, and Ellen J. Langer. "Sex, Age, and Smartphone Addiction Across 41 Countries." *International Journal of Mental Health and Addiction Article* (2023). https://doi.org/10.1007/s11469-023-01146 -3. See also Jonathan Haidt, *The Anxious Generation* (New York: Penguin Press, 2024), which probes the impacts that screen time exacts on young people.

18 C. Montag, B. Lachmann, M. Herrlich, and K. Zweig. "Addictive Features of Social Media/Messenger Platforms and Freemium Games against the Background of Psychological and Economic Theories." *Int J Environ Res Public Health* 16, no. 14 (2019): 2612. https://doi.org/10.3390/ ijerph16142612.

19 While "awareness" might seem like a departure from the conventional translations of the word "*zehirut*" as "caution" or "watchfulness," in fact, awareness is the active process required in order to be cautious or watchful. The linguistic basis for this translation is the fact that the root of the word *zehirut* is Z-H-R, which means "bright" and, in this context, "bright consciousness" or awareness.

Chapter 1

1 זהירות.

2 Its root letters are *zayin-heh-resh*.

3 Daniel 12:3; Ezekiel 8:2.

4 Hunt. *Murshid.* quoted in *Routledge Handbook on Sufism.*

5 The first major written collection of the Jewish oral traditions was redacted by Rabbi Judah HaNasi between the end of the second and the beginning of the third centuries.

6 Exodus 35:3.

7 Electricity did not exist when the rules of Shabbat were established, of course, and so when electricity became readily available, the rabbis debated how it should be understood and categorized. There were different opinions, but in the end, electricity was equated to fire, and turning on or off a device to *kindling or extinguishing a flame,* and that made its use a violation of the biblical prohibition on lighting a fire on the Sabbath.

8 Exodus 20:8.

9 Deuteronomy 5:12.

10 For the full list and details on each of the thirty-nine: https://halachipedia .com/index.php?title=Index_of_Laws_of_Shabbat_by_the_39_Melachot.

11 a *chatat;* a sin offering.

Chapter 2

1 Dessler, *Strive for Truth!; Michtav Me'Eliyahu,* II: 13.

2 Originally from Australia, he is an instructor at Yeshiva University and an alumnus of Neve Yerushalayim College.

3 *Menucha* was also the name of the country estate of Julius Meier, the son of Jewish immigrants who built a thriving department store business and was elected the twentieth governor of the state of Oregon. He gave his estate the name *Menucha,* by which it is still known to this day. It was at *Menucha* where Meier entered his own final rest in 1937.

4 Exodus 20:10.

5 Exodus 23:12.

6 Strong's Concordance, entry 5314.

7 Adin Steinsaltz, *The Thirteen Petalled Rose* (New York: Basic Books, 1980), 132. Translated by Yehuda Hanegbi, Basic Books, New York.

8 The name Noah in Hebrew is *Noach*, which is linguistically related to the word *menucha*.

9 *Madreigat HaAdam*, quoted in "Cheshvan: To Achieve Serenity." *Mishpacha Magazine*, October 14, 2020.

10 Rabbi Simcha Zissel Ziv, known as the Alter of Kelm (1824–1898).

11 *Daat Torah, Bereishit*, 148. Also see *Daat Chochma u'Mussar*, volume 2, essay 65.

12 The Jubilee, from the Hebrew *yovel*, is the fiftieth year that follows the passage of seven cycles of sabbatical years, or forty-nine total years. This fiftieth year is a "reset" when land, property, and property rights, including over other people, are returned to their original settings.

13 Berachot 57b.

14 Based on a contemplation offered by Rabbi Avi Fertig in *Bridging the Gap*, 508.

15 I am indebted to Rabbi Avi Fertig for this idea. See chapters 40–41 of *Bridging the Gap*.

16 Dessler, *Strive for Truth!; Michtav Me'Eliyahu*, IV: 4.

17 Adin Steinsaltz, Daniel Haberman, and Yehudit Shabta. *Change & Renewal: The Essence of the Jewish Holidays, Festivals and Days of Remembrance*, 1st Eng. ed. (New Milford, CT; Jerusalem: Maggid Books, 2011).

18 Oliver Sacks. "Oliver Sacks: Sabbath." *The New York Times*, August 14, 2015. https://www.nytimes.com/2015/08/16/opinion/sunday/oliver-sacks-sabbath.html.

19 Shlomo Wolbe, *Alei Shur: Volume 1* (Jerusalem: Bais Hamussar, 1985), 194. Jerusalem, Israel.

20 Management-Issues.com. "Why You Need Equanimity." http://www.management-issues.com/opinion/5992/why-you-need-equanimity/ (accessed December 10, 2024).

21 Solomon Breuer and Joseph Breuer. *[Ḥokhmah u-Musar] = Chochmo u'mussar: An Original Approach to Sidrah Interpretation. 2,* One-Volume ed. Divre Shelomoh (Jerusalem; New York: Feldheim, 1996), 255.

22 Menachem Mendel Leffin. *Cheshbon Hanefesh* (Jerusalem; New York: Feldheim, 1995), 109.

23 Herman Wouk. *This Is My God: The Jewish Way of Life.* 1st ed. A Back Bay Book Theology (Boston: Little, Brown, 1988).

Chapter 3

1 From the root: ס–פ–ק that also gives rise to the commonly used Hebrew word "*maspik;*" enough.

2 Sanhedrin 107a.

3 1872–1970; Poland, England, and Israel.

4 Rabbi Yitzchok Tzvi Schwarz. "I Have Everything." *Yated.Com*, November 17, 2021. https://yated.com/i-have-everything/.

5 *Chapters of First Principles*, composed in Israel around 200 CE, is the only book of the legal text called the Mishnah that contains almost no laws, consisting instead of short statements of advice, ethics, and wisdom.

6 *Pirkei Avot* 4:1.

7 Translated by Rabbi Shraga Silverstein. (New York & Jerusalem: Moznaim Publishing Corp, 1994), 282.

8 *Kohelet Rabbah* 1:13.

9 Numbers 4–6.

10 Moses ben Maimon, commonly known as Maimonides and also referred to by the acronym Rambam (1138–1204).

11 *Moreh Nevuchim [Guide to the Perplexed]* 3:12 to Exodus 16:18.

12 Gladiator GarageWorks. "Almost 1 in 4 Americans Say Their Garage Is Too Cluttered to Fit Their Car." June 09, 2015. https://www.prnewswire.com/news-releases/almost-1-in-4-americans-say-their-garage-is-too-cluttered-to-fit-their-car-300096246.html.

13 Jeanne E. Arnold. *Life at Home in the Twenty-First Century: 32 Families Open Their Doors* (Los Angeles: Cotsen Institute of Archaeology at UCLA, 2012).

14 Emilie Le Beau Lucchesi. "The Unbearable Heaviness of Clutter." *The New York Times*, January 3, 2019. https://www.nytimes.com/2019/01/03/well/mind/clutter-stress-procrastination-psychology.html.

15 OLEM US EPA. "National Overview: Facts and Figures on Materials, Wastes and Recycling." Overviews and Factsheets, October 2, 2017. https://www.epa.gov/facts-and-figures-about-materials-waste-and-recycling/national-overview-facts-and-figures-materials.

16 Amy Freeman. "Do You Know What's Happening to Your Clothing Donations?" *The Washington Post*, January 28, 2020. https://www.washingtonpost.com/lifestyle/home/whats-in-your-landfill-lots-of-textiles/2020/01/27/7d43830c-364c-11ea-bb7b-265f4554af6d_story.html.

17 As stated in many sources, including the Midrash, *Otiot d'Rabbi Akiva* [*The Letters of Rabbi Akiva*], that is a commentary on God's creation of the universe through the Hebrew alphabet.

18 Genesis 2:2.

19 ויכל.

20 כל.

21 As pointed out in Bava Batra 17a: *"Bakol"* occurs in reference to Abraham in Genesis 24:1; *"mikol"* refers to a later quote about Isaac (Genesis 27:33), and *"kol"* a subsequent quote about Jacob (Genesis 33:11).

22 Genesis 33:11.

23 Genesis 33:9.

24 Bava Batra 16b.

25 *"U'v'tuvo mechadeish b'chol yom tamid ma'aseh bereishit."*

26 *"l'Oseh orim gedolim, ki l'olam chasdo"*; Psalms. 136:7.

27 Carl Zimmer. "This Mutant Crayfish Clones Itself, and It's Taking Over Europe." *The New York Times*, February 5, 2018. https://www.nytimes.com/2018/02/05/science/mutant-crayfish-clones-europe.html.

28 Exodus 20:9.

29 Citing an older source, a midrash: Mekhilta d'Rabbi Yishmael 20:9.

30 לשֶׁבֶת; *lashevet.*

31 Born in Malaga, Spain, about 1021; died about 1058 in Valencia.

32 1892–1953; Lithuania, England, and Israel.

33 *Strive for Truth!*, vol. 4, ed. Aryeh Carmel (New York: Feldheim Publishers, 2002), 4. New York and Jerusalem.

Chapter 4

1 The Torah instructs: *v'samachta b'chagecha*; "you shall be joyful in your festival" (Deuteronomy 16:14).

2 Sifrei 77; to that verse.

3 *Halachot Gedolot* ("Great Laws"), written by Rabbi Simeon Kayyara (the *Bahag*).

4 Isaiah 58:13.

5 In the introduction to the section on joy in my book, *Every Day, Holy Day*, 5.

6 Irving Greenberg. *The Jewish Way: Living the Holidays* (New York: Touchstone, 1993), 129.

7 All Jewish formulations of the anatomy of the soul include *nefesh* and *neshama* and also a third dimension, the *ruach*, that does not concern us here. Other schemes include two higher levels, the *chiya* and the *yechida*.

8 *Zohar*, Tzav 29b.

9 Genesis 2:3.

10 *Genesis Rabbah* 11:2.

11 *Alei Shur*, vol. 2, 382.

12 Shabbat 118b.

13 *Princess Sabbath*, trans. Margaret Armour, 1851.

14 *Ohr HaTzafun*, Vol. III, 84.

15 *Ohr HaTzafun*, Vol. II, 122.

16 "When the Temple is standing, *the altar atones for a person; now it is a person's table that atones for him.*" Talmud Hagiga 27a.

17 *Mishneh Torah*, Shabbat 30:14.

18 Quoted in R. Shlomo Yosef Zevin, in his *Soferim U-Sefarim*, 130.

Chapter 5

1 *Genesis Rabbah* 38:6.

2 Hebrew is a gender-binary language. I have heard of a gender-neutral version of this greeting, which is: "*mah sh'lomchol?*"

3 Based on the name Gideon gave to an altar ("YHVH-Shalom") in Judges 6:24, the rabbis conclude that "the name of God is 'Peace'" (*Perek ha'Shalom*, Shabbat 10b).

4 Derived from the verses in Numbers 6:23–27.

5 Shabbat 23b.

6 There is a third category as well, which is *bein adam l'Makom*, between a person and God.

7 Cited in *Living Shabbos* by Rabbi David Sutton, ArtScroll / Mesorah Publications Ltd.

8 If there is an author to this story, that person is unknown to me. I have heard versions of this story in so many contexts that it seems to me it merits being called "traditional."

9 *Genesis Rabbah* 85:4: "One who begins to perform a commandment and does not complete it buries his wife and sons."

10 The Talmud (Bava Metzia 58b) teaches that insulting a person in public is tantamount to murdering them. The rabbis draw an association between the white face of embarrassment and the white face of a corpse. "Anyone who humiliates another in public, it is as though he were spilling blood."

11 Numbers 30:3: "If a person makes a vow to the Lord or takes an oath imposing an obligation on himself, he shall not break his pledge; he must carry out all that has crossed his lips."

12 Exodus 35:3.

13 Leviticus 24:23.

14 Vol. 2, 89b.

15 *Princess Sabbath*, trans. Margaret Armour, 1851.

16 *Avot d'Rabbi Natan* 28:3.

17 Yoma 72b.

Chapter 6

1 Kate Wagner. "City Noise Might Be Making You Sick." *The Atlantic* (blog), February 20, 2018. https://www.theatlantic.com/technology/archive/2018 /02/city-noise-might-be-making-you-sick/553385/.

2 Quoting the *Yalkut Shimoni*, Beha'alotkha.

3 King Solomon, to whom the book of Proverbs is attributed.

4 Proverbs 10:19.

5 The Long Search, documentary series, directed by Ronald Eyre (United Kingdom: BBC, 1977).

6 *Chapters of First Principles*, 1:17.

7 Proverbs 18:21.

8 Proverbs 21:23.

9 Peter Cole, *The Dream of the Poem: Hebrew Poetry from Muslim and Christian Spain, 950–1492* (Princeton: Princeton University Press, 2007), 199. New Haven.

10 *Orot HaKodesh*, III, 273. Abraham Isaac Kook (1865–1935) was a Jewish thinker and legal scholar considered one of the most important sources of modern Religious Zionism.

11 "By the word of God, the heavens were made; and by the breath of God's mouth, all of their host" (Psalm 33:6).

12 The *Baruch Sh'amar* prayer.

13 Genesis 2:7.

14 *ruach memalela*.

15 Arachin 15b.

16 "*Wondrous Counsel*," written by Rabbi Eliezer Papo and first published in Constantinople in 1824, 363.

17 *Every Day, Holy Day*, 169.

18 *Chotam Tochnit* (Amsterdam, 1864), 261. Levisson.

19 Psalm 46:10.

20 *Exodus Rabbah* 29:9.

21 In *Derech HaChaim*, commentary to *Pirkei Avot* 1:17.

22 *Pirkei Avot*, often incorrectly translated as "Chapters of the Fathers."

23 1937–2024.

24 Rabbi David Sutton. "Friday Afternoon—Danger Zone!" *Kosher.com*, September 6, 2018. https://www.kosher.com/article/friday-afternoon-danger-zone-468/.

Chapter 7

1 See, Daniel Stein. "The Limits of Religious Optimism: The Hazon Ish and the Alter of Novardok on Bittahon." *Tradition: A Journal of Orthodox Jewish Thought* 43, no. 2 (summer 2010), 31–48. Available online at https://traditiononline.org/the-limits-of-religious-optimism-the-hazon-ish-and-the-alter-of-novardok-on-bittahon/

2 Ruchama Shain. *All for the Boss* (New York: Feldheim, 2001). New York and Jerusalem.

3 *Da'at Chochmah u'Mussar*, 1.

4 Rabbi Avrohom Yeshaya Karelitz (1878–1953).

5 Yevamot 63b quotes the book of Ben Sira, a second-century BCE Jerusalem sage who authored an apocryphal poetic book of guidance for living a wise, ethical, and God-fearing life.

6 Leticia Miranda. "America's Orthodox Jews Are Selling a Ton of the Products You Buy on Amazon." *BuzzFeed News*, September 4, 2019. https://www.buzzfeednews.com/article/leticiamiranda/amazon-orthodox-jews.

7 *Yalkut Shimoni*, Psalms 643.

8 *Yalkut Shimoni*, Psalms 719.

9 Rabbi *Yechezkel Levenstein* (Rav Yechezkel HaLevi Levenstein), known as Reb Chatzkel (1885–1974), was the *mashgiach ruchani* (spiritual supervisor) of the Mir yeshiva.

10 *Sefer Ohr Yechezkiel.*

11 Immanuel Etkes, *Rabbi Israel Salanter and the Musar Movement* (Jerusalem: Jewish Publication Society, 1993), 61.

12 *Sefer HaIkarim* 4:47.

13 Berachot 60b.

14 Melissa Chan, "Here's How Winning the Lottery Makes You Miserable." *TIME*, January 12, 2016. https://time.com/4176128/powerball-jackpot-lottery-winners/.

15 Commentary to Proverbs 3:26.

16 See also Maharal (*Netivot Olam*, "Netiv Ha'Bitachon"): "How powerful is the trait of *bitachon*, that when one trusts in God with all one's heart so that all the events that happen are considered favorable—as with Rabbi Akiva—and when one trusts in God, it is upon God to save him."

17 *Peh Kadosh* (Jerusalem: Makhon Moreshet Ha-Yeshivot, 1994), 235.

18 Berachot 35b.

19 *rabbim.*

20 Exodus 16:27.

21 *Even Shleimah*, Chapter 3.

Chapter 8

1 Leviticus 19:2.

2 Preface to *Lights of Holiness*, 18; my translation.

3 Leviticus 23:1–2.

4 Exodus 28:36.

5 Genesis 2:2.

6 Exodus 34:21.

7 Pesachim 106a.

8 Psalm 104:15.

9 Hosea 4:11.

10 Jewish law forbids making the blessing over wine that is still in the bottle unless there is absolutely no cup of any kind to be had.

11 Exodus 3:5.

12 The Hebrew word for conscience is *matzpun* and the word for compass is *matzpen*, revealing the utility of the conscience for orienting our lives.

13 *Strive for Truth!*, vol. 4, 7; insertion in square brackets in the original.

14 Jerusalem Talmud, Shabbat 15.3.

15 *Ohr HaTzafun*, Part 1, 123.

16 *Strive for Truth!*, vol. 6, 6.

17 *Shemonah K'vatzim*, Notebook 2: Entry 35.

Conclusion

1 Born in Berlin in 1914; died in Jerusalem in 2005. Author of *Alei Shur*.

2 *Alei Shur*, vol. 1, 194.

3 Psalm 92:12–15.

Bibliographic Essay

Primary Sources

Anonymous. *Ways of the Righteous*, translated by Shraga Silverstein. New York and Jerusalem: Feldheim, 1995.

Written in Germany the mid-1500s and originally titled *Book of Character Traits*, it was retitled *Orchot Tzaddikim* (*Ways of the Righteous*) by a later copyist. This popular handbook of Jewish behavioural codes is not so much original thought as a compilation of biblical sources that delineate the ideals toward which a human being should strive, character trait by character trait.

Blazer, Rabbi Yitzchak. *Light of Israel*, translated by Rabbis Irving (Yitz) Greenberg and Justin Pines. New Milford and Jerusalem: Koren Publishers, 2024.

Ohr Yisrael was compiled in 1890 by the chief disciple of Rabbi Yisrael Salanter, founder of the 19th century Mussar movement, and includes Rabbi Salanter's Mussar Epistle and other writings along with Rabbi Blazer's teachings and memoirs. The text explores how a purely intellectual approach to self-improvement can blind people to the hidden impulses that drive behaviour, and advocates for addressing subconscious and irrational motives in any effort to improve characters and service to God.

Cordovero, Rabbi Moses. *Palm Tree of Deborah*, translated by Moshe Miller. Southfield, MI: Targum, 1994.

Originally published in Hebrew as *Tomer Devorah*, which translates literally as *Palm Tree of Deborah*, this small book was written in Tzfat in the 16th century. It identifies interpersonal relationships as the key arena in which personal spiritual development can take place, and it finds a model in the loving—but challenging—relationship that exists between Israel and God.

Dessler, Rabbi Eliyahu. *Strive for Truth!* translated by Aryeh Carmel. New York and Jerusalem: Feldheim, 1978.

This six-volume series is an English translation of some of the writings of Rabbi Eliyahu Dessler (1892–1953) the great-grandson of Rabbi Israel Salanter,

originally published in Hebrew as *Michtav Me'Eliyahu*, literally "Letter
from Elijah." Rav Dessler was trained in the traditional Lithuanian Mussar
but because he lived in England from 1928 to 1949, his writings address a
modern, western community, and are a bridge back to the traditional world
from which he came.

ibn Rabbi Bahya Paquda. *Duties of the Heart*, translated by Daniel Haberman.
New York and Jerusalem: Feldheim, 1996.

Originally written in Spain in Judea-Arabic around 1080 and translated into
Hebrew about a century later, this pillar of the Mussar tradition explores
spiritual life in a down-to-earth, comprehensive and accessible manner.
Structured as ten "gates" that examine the ten fundamental principles which,
according to Bahya, constitute human spiritual life, topics include God's
unity (a more philosophical treatise often skipped by Mussar teachers), faith
and trust in God, human suffering, repentance, providence, the soul, and
more.

Leffin, Rabbi Menachem Mendel of Satanov. *Accounting of the Soul*, translated
by Dovid Landesman. New York and Jerusalem: Feldheim, 1996.

Cheshbon HaNefesh (Accounting of the Soul) was written in 1809 by Rabbi
Menachem Mendel Leffin (1749–1826) to propound a system of character
development that some have speculated was derived from Benjamin
Franklin. He offers an innovative, step-by-step program for character
refinement that was so valuable that in 1845, Rabbi Yisrael Salanter
encouraged a group of students to republish it with a foreword by Rabbi
Yitzchok Isaak Sher of Slobodka. One of his innovations in this book was to
introduce journaling to the practice of Mussar.

Luzzatto, Moshe Chaim. *The Complete Mesillat Yesharim in Two Versions:
Dialogue and Thematic*, translated by Avraham Shoshanna. Cleveland: Ofeq
Institute, 2007.

In 1740, after having been exiled from his native Italy to Amsterdam, Rabbi
Luzzatto (known as Ramchal; 1707–1746) published this masterwork of
Mussar, titled in English as *Path of the Just*. Widely learned in virtually
every yeshiva since formal study of Mussar texts was introduced to the
yeshiva curriculum under the influence of the Musar Movement, it is almost
unique in the Jewish world in having found favour as well in Chassidic
and Kabbalistic circles. The aim is character improvement, and the author
explores how key traits can be acquired, and what might hinder their
acquisition.

Maimon, Rabbi Moses ben (Maimonides; Rambam). *Eight Chapters*, translated
by Rabbi Yaakov Feldman. Southfield, MI: Targum. 2008.

Written as an introduction to the primary source of Jewish ethics, *Pirkei
Avot*, the *Eight Chapters* (*Shemonah Perakim*) has long been considered an

essential source for Jewish thought and ethics. Touching on core beliefs, ethics and principles of character development, it stands as a guide to our relationship with God, direction in relating to others, and insight into understanding and transforming ourselves.

Papo, Rabbi Eliezer. *Pele Yoetz.* Rahway, NJ: Mesorah Publications. 2023.

Organized by topic in alphabetical order, this text is an encyclopedia of Jewish ethics, prayer, behavior, guidance, and thought that was authored by the legal authority, ethicist, and kabbalist Rabbi Eliezer Papo (1785–1826) of present-day Bulgaria. Every entry teaches and discusses a key element of the inner life, drawing on a wide variety of traditional Jewish sources as well as the author's insightful awareness of human nature.

Secondary Sources

Etkes, Immanuel. *Rabbi Israel Salanter and the Mussar Movement: Seeking the Torah of Truth,* translated by Jonathan Chipman. Philadelphia and Jerusalem: Jewish Publication Society, 1993.

An historian from the Hebrew University, Professor Etkes provides a comprehensive account of the formative 19th century Mussar movement, including its sources, context, leading exponents, teachings and impact.

Goldberg, Hillel. *Israel Salanter: Text, Structure, Idea.* New York: KTAV, 1982.

This scholarly work offers a detailed and thorough investigation of Rabbi Salanter's wide-ranging and influential thought by tracking the development of his ideas and practices through a succession of periods.

Morinis, Alan. *Everyday Holiness.* Boston: Trumpeter, 2007.

My own guide to the practical teachings of Mussar toward cultivating personal change and spiritual growth in the midst of day-to-day life.

Morinis, Alan. *With Heart in Mind.* Boston: Trumpeter, 2014.

A further exploration of a wide range of Mussar sources and insights, organized according to the 48 pathways for the acquisition of Torah outlined in Pirkei Avot 6:6.

Index

Note: Page numbers followed by "n" refer to notes.

About the Author

Alan Morinis, founder of the Mussar Institute, is a leading figure in the contemporary revival of the Mussar movement, a 1,100-year-old authentic Jewish personal and communal spiritual tradition. A Rhodes Scholar and anthropologist, he reached a personal turning point in his life in 1997 that led him to seek out the late Rabbi Yechiel Yitzchok Perr, an accomplished master who stood in an unbroken line of transmission of the Mussar tradition.

Following years of study, he reinterpreted the ancient Mussar learnings and practices for modern audiences in *Climbing Jacob's Ladder* (2002) and *Everyday Holiness* (2007). To address the growing public interest in Mussar, he founded The Mussar Institute in 2004. He went on to author two more books, *Every Day, Holy Day* (2010) and *With Heart in Mind* (2014). Alan lives in Vancouver, British Columbia, and continues to explore and interpret original Mussar sources in Hebrew and is making these valuable teachings available to the contemporary world.